manboobs

manboobs

a memoir of musicals, visas, hope, and cake

komail aijazuddin

abrams press, new york

Library of Congress Control Number: 2024935814

ISBN: 978-1-4197-7384-6
eISBN: 979-8-88707-293-7

Printed and bound in the United States
10 9 8 7 6 5 4 3 2 1

Some names and identifying characteristics have been changed,
and some dialogue has been re-created.

Abrams books are available at special discounts when purchased in quantity for
premiums and promotions as well as fundraising or educational use. Special editions can
also be created to specification. For details, contact specialsales@abramsbooks.com or
the address below.

Abrams Press® is a registered trademark of Harry N. Abrams, Inc.

ABRAMS The Art of Books
195 Broadway, New York, NY 10007
abramsbooks.com

I dedicate this book to you, with the hope that in reading my story you may find the strength to tell your own.

Our love is God.

from *Heathers: The Musical*

CONTENTS

AUTHOR'S NOTE

By the time you reach the tap-dancing breasts, you will probably have pieced together that this book is more than a mere retelling of my life. Names and identifying characteristics have been changed and some conversations have been re-created from memory. Please accept the following pages as more true than real. Now that we've dispensed with business, let me just say: Hello, welcome, I love what you're wearing, and I've been waiting to meet you for a very long time.

PROLOGUE

"*T*ITS AND ASS!" I SANG, mimicking the blond dancer on-screen singing about her breast augmentation. "Can change your life! They sure changed mine!"

"Perhaps," my grandmother said from behind her steaming tea cup, "*A Chorus Line* isn't an appropriate movie for a four-year-old."

"He just likes the dancing," my mother assured her as I pranced off our dining table in perfect synchronicity to the lyrics "debutante or chorus girl or wife."

Like many gay boys (we sometimes answer to "old souls"), I adored dance movies growing up, but *A Chorus Line*, that Lycra love letter to leg warmers, was singularly fabulous. A movie version of the hit 1970s Broadway musical, *A Chorus Line* tells the daylong story of a group of backup dancers auditioning for their big break in front of a famous choreographer played by Michael Douglas, who doesn't dance in the film but still looks mortified through most of it anyway.

I spent years perfecting my lip sync to the blond girl's racy number "Dance: Ten, Looks: Three," my favorite from the soundtrack not simply because the song has the phrase "tits and ass" in it but also because the woman in the movie who sang it wore a flesh-toned bikini, high heels, and, for reasons best explained by the 1980s, a black buckled belt. I desperately wanted to be her. But other than mosquitoes, Lahore had no real leg warmers to speak of, and so I'd strip down to my Superman underwear and secretly wear my mother's silver stilettos over an old pair of fuchsia woolen socks that slumped around my ankles with pleasing period-piece accuracy.

"Perhaps a cartoon *would* be better," my mother said.

A Chorus Line was a holy text ever relevant no matter my age, which I suppose is often the case with adult movies one sees young. I was eight, for instance, before I learned that "Dance: Ten, Looks: Three" was actually a song about body dysmorphia and not, as I'd suspected, an ode to young motherhood; it wasn't until acne slapped me that I realized the youngest dancer singing the word "gonorrhea" as a Gregorian chant was really singing about puberty; and it took an argument with a woman dressed as a carrot at a 50 Cent concert in Montreal for me to finally recognize the character who falls down in the third act was a drag queen. The movie holds up. Even now, whenever I watch the ensemble cast singing in harmony about having sex in a graveyard interrupted only by saxophone solos and wisps of hairspray, I think, *What child wouldn't love this?*

My favorite character wasn't Ms. Tits, though; it was Sheila, the ancient thirty-year-old dancer who took aspirins by wee fistfuls and chain-smoked with blow-dried abandon. Sheila reminded me of the women I saw around me in Pakistan, those thin-lipped, well-coiffed, razor-tongued aunties who sat morosely at dinner parties puffing mutinously on their tenth Silk Cut in cynical silence, both prisoners and patrons of our shared patriarchal penitentiary. Sheila too had that look of resigned depression buttressed by designer perfume.

My early exposure to American musical theatre—in the name of the *Fiddler*, *The Phantom*, and *The Wiz*, amen—was probably a result of my parents' relative age rather than any deliberate curation, but I happily grew up on a diet of old Hollywood musicals and original cast recordings. It later came as a slight shock to discover how much of a gay cliché my interests were considered when I finally moved abroad, but my deep familiarity with Broadway tunes freaked out enough white gay men to be well worth the time.

"How did you even watch *A Chorus Line* in Pakistan?" a hipster named something unforgivable like Hunter might ask me in a dimly lit Brooklyn restaurant. From his expression you'd think I just revealed I ran a low-end wine bar in Kabul called Bacon 'n' Booze.

"We had VCRs in Pakistan . . ."

"Isn't Pakistan against, you know . . . musicals?" This he whispered with a worried sideways glance, as if an errant suicide bomber was mere moments away from jumping out from behind the retro jukebox with the words *Death to Liza* scrawled in Arabic across his angry forehead in blood and lipstick.

"Only *Starlight Express*," I replied, but Hunter didn't get the joke.

Of course, what he was really asking was: "How were you gay in Pakistan?"

But after twenty years in and out of New York City, I also recognized the more fundamental prejudices hiding behind his incredulity: When did you begin your journey to our deliverance? How did you see the light of our rainbow from inside one of those dark brown countries that hate freedoms? Where does a gay-brown-Pakistani-American man like you fit in here anyway? Are you with us or against us?

No one likes to be reduced to a string of epithets to explain their infinite splendor, but to paraphrase Toni Morrison, everyone has to hyphenate in America unless you're white. Hyphens are the price of my admission through the gates of the American dream, and also why after two decades I still feel perpetually outside its vague but promised deliverance. I grew up being told I was too gay to be Pakistani, so I left, only to be told I was too Pakistani to be gay. Eventually I reconciled that no matter how many Broadway tunes I knew or pop culture references I recognized, a vital part of me would never be accepted, no matter where in the world I was.

I'm not sure when exactly in my childhood I internalized the belief that it was fundamentally wrong for me to find love, but in the late eighties the world was as hostile to queers as it was to minimalist makeup. TV and movies both assured me that the answer to the unending question of my gayness—the answer to any question, really—was waiting in the United States of America. There, and only there, would I be free, accepted, and loved. It would take three decades, two passports, and an unfortunate perm to discover that homophobia is no more a problem solved by geography than any other kind of hatred, and in the meantime I unwittingly carried the weight of other people's expectations wherever I went (yes, Hunter, even into Brooklyn). It's taken my entire life to learn how to put that weight down, and it will take the rest of my life to keep it there.

So, if you must know how I "loved musicals" in Pakistan, the question you're really asking is how I found the courage to be myself no matter where I was. The short answer is "exquisite tailoring." The long answer is in your hands.

Chapter 1

SINGULAR SENSATION

"*T's my toy!*" I shouted, but Tara snatched the tiny plastic mermaid out of my hand and squatted in the corner of her room like a venomous toad.

"You shouldn't even *have* a mermaid doll!" Tara snarled. "Mermaids are for girls. Are you a *girl*?"

"It's still mine," I reminded her for the record. There is always a record.

"I'm going to tell everyone you're a girl then!" she said. "Komail is a girl! Komail is a girl! Komail is a girl!"

"You're adopted," I said, watching helplessly as Tara mangled the mermaid fins I'd spent the last half hour molding into an arc of graceful whimsy. "I hope you know that."

The surly spawn of family friends, Tara was my only playmate when we first moved to Lahore, but even at five she was an insufferable little shit. I tolerated her because playing with Tara allowed me unfettered access to everything a girly gay boy could need but never buy: *Rainbow Brite* cassette tapes, My Little Pony figurines, Disney princess makeup tables, a sorority of Barbies, and even a Malibu dollhouse complete with sun deck and the optional jacuzzi. Tara's company was the abusive price I paid for access to these wonderful things, not unlike the inane conversations one has to endure with talkative pot dealers at college ("No, Kyle, no one actually cares what you think about communism. Put the weed on the table and fuck off back to your incense sticks"). Tara would unleash torrential temper tantrums if I so much as looked at her toys, and her nanny, an early believer that screens make the best babysitters, always suggested a movie to calm things down.

"No!" Tara screamed. "I don't want *him* to choose the movie."

"Tara!" said the nanny in a honey-dipped voice. "Be nice to your guest and you can have some ice cream!"

"OK," Tara said later, glaring at me from behind two scoops of chocolate gelato. "Which cartoon do you want to watch, *guest*?"

Like most elections in Pakistan, movie time was a rigged event, and so this next bit took some planning and not a small amount of thespian commitment.

"Let me think . . . what could we watch today . . . hmmm . . . something with fighting, of course . . . and it *has* to have guns . . . perhaps tanks . . . oh, I know! Why don't we see . . . *G.I. Joe*!" I already knew that Tara hated army cartoons, despite the bowl cut that made her look like a Russian henchman named Boris.

"NO!" she screamed. "No! No! No! I want to see—"

"Don't say *The Little Mermaid*!" I moaned, clutching my ears like an extra in *Doctor Zhivago* wailing against the bitter injustices of this cold life. "Don't you dare say *The Little Mermaid*. Please not *The Little Mermaid*. ANYTHING BUT *THE LITTLE MERMAID*!"

"I want to see," Tara said, her boss eye aflame with cruelty, "*The Little Mermaid*!"

Bull's-eye.

Obviously, Tara wasn't the brightest bulb in the chandelier. She grew up to develop a buffet of eating disorders and eventually married a closeted gay man, but I'm getting ahead of myself.

After the cartoon, we reenacted the best bits, Tara wrapping a red towel around her head to play Ariel because "it's my house" and me having to play the hunky but problematic Prince Eric, forced to chase her in mock desire as she wriggled on the carpet like a leech with a sex addiction. But it wasn't until we got to the parts of the villainous plus-size Queen of Calamari that is Ursula the sea witch that I could give my truly command performances.

"One shouldn't lurk in doorways," I'd purr in my huskiest drawl, unfurling myself from behind the bathroom door with aquatic grace. "It's . . . rrrrrrrrrrude." Tara would scream and run to hide in her parents' room, finally leaving me alone in the spotlight to sing the entirety of "Poor Unfortunate Souls" to her now utterly terrified caregiver.

Like *A Chorus Line*'s Sheila, Ursula the sea witch was a beloved early addition to my personal pantheon of strong women with smoker's coughs. Maybe it was because Disney had based her character on the real-life drag queen Divine; or maybe it was because, like me, she too was voluminously fat, wildly misunderstood, and had a manic fondness for other people's accessories. Whatever it was, watching her tentacles float across my screen, I felt a ping of familiarity that bordered on the supernatural. When Ursula tries to electrocute Ariel at the end of the movie for reneging on their contractually binding agreement, I'd always think, *Now that's a woman who knows her worth.*

Every queer person born before 2010 had to be a self-taught cultural archaeologist as a child, forced as we were to sift through compacted layers of heterocentric history to excavate even the tiniest glints of queer representation. Most of the time there weren't any, which made discoveries like Ursula magical and vital. We often found versions of ourselves in the camp villains of Disney—Maleficent, Scar, Jafar, Gaston and his chest hair—since they, like us, were gay jesters of nonconformity in an otherwise drab court of appeasers.

It would take some time for me to realize we were always the villains in their fairy tales.

Disney cartoons offered me an immediate escape from the rigidity of my new surroundings in Pakistan. I was not nearly as scared of my family's move to Lahore in 1989 as I should have been. Born and raised in Abu Dhabi until age five, I spent my earliest years thinking of Pakistan as the hot, humid place I traveled to once a year to visit my grandparents. My parents had moved to the United Arab Emirates with their two daughters in the seventies—one small drop in the wave of South Asians (Pakistanis, Indians, Sri Lankans, Bangladeshis) who began arriving in the UAE as the country's oil exports boomed and its economy flourished. Gulf oil states like the UAE embody the diet cola of capitalist aspirations, a first world lite, if you will. Living there allows all the economic trappings of a developed nation without any of the human rights, not that most people who lived there minded. Yes, you were under the rule of despotic absolute monarchies, but there was also a Burger King, so, you know, choices.

By 1989, Pakistan was still teetering out of the decade-long oppressive rule of an evil military dictator obsessed with imposing hard-line Islamic ideologies on everything except his eyebrows. It was he and his political heirs who made sure the country became a repressive place where girls didn't feel safe, you couldn't kiss anyone in public, and there wasn't a single Burger King.

Kings had much to do with my father's family's sense of identity. His side was a large and motley clan of jaded aristocrats addicted to sniffing the potent fumes of a storied but distant past. The family traced their superiority complexes back to a seventeenth-century trio of courtier brothers who served as royal advisors to the king of Lahore, a one-eyed Sikh man named Maharaja Ranjit Singh. My great-aunt *khala* Boob (shortened by family from her real name, the longer but admittedly far less suggestive Mahboob) retold the family name origin story whenever I was forced to visit her art deco mansion for Sunday tea. So pleased was the maharaja with the fierce loyalty of the three Muslim brothers in his court, *khala* Boob recounted with pride, that he offered to bestow on their family a title of great rank so that they may be honored for all time.

"So, what kind of a name would you like?" the maharaja asked.

"Give us a title that humbles us when we are rich," the brothers told him, "and lifts us when we are poor." Sadly this didn't leave much wiggle room, with the result that every male member of my father's line carries the title *fakir*, a word that literally translates to "beggar," as the kids on the Lahori playground told me shortly after we arrived.

"It actually means 'ascetic,'" I explained between punches, but they didn't care. I bristled at having to haul a caravan of conspicuously unusual names behind me just because I was a boy, especially since both my older sisters got away with only two names, like normal kids ("kids" is a stretch; my closest sibling is nearly a decade older). I've often wondered since then how *khala* Boob reconciled her obvious pride of our family name with the institutional misogyny that meant she was never actually allowed to use it herself. I never asked her, and she would probably have told me to piss off if I did. My grandparents divorced in the fifties (escándalo!), and my father was very young when he and his siblings were sent off to an expensive private boarding school in a very racist postwar England thousands of miles away from home. Those early traumas might make some sense of his inextinguishable desire to root himself in the city of his ancestors, but I knew none of this as we landed in Lahore for our new life and was consequently resentful.

"Oh, look!" my mother said as she gestured out of the plane window to the dusty gray-green sprawl of Lahore below. "It's so green!"

As if one could befriend a eucalyptus tree.

My mother never wanted to move to Lahore. Few people from Karachi ever do. Well-read, beautiful, and thirsty for global experiences, she looked down on the city as a pustule of Punjabi provincialism and feudal posturing. We all grew up thinking of Ma as a bit psychic, so perhaps she already knew back then the move would force her into decades of inane conversation with women who never read and men who never listened.

Thankfully, both my parents recognized that to send me straight from a day care run by cockney hippies in Abu Dhabi into the Pakistani local school system would be tantamount to child abuse, so I was initially enrolled in a local but internationally stocked kindergarten at the American school. The school catered to the children of a handful of foreign expats posted in Lahore (my first fight was with a five-year-old German lesbian over who was closer friends with Akari, the extremely chic Japanese girl who gave everyone kisses and, subsequently, chicken pox. I was more interested in Willam, the hunky Australian TA). We spent our mornings playing "show-and-tell" and taking power naps between chocolate milk breaks. It was a short-lived heaven. A year later, I was enrolled in the first grade at my father's old all-boys school across the canal: the Academy.

Situated in a devastatingly beautiful but toxically repressive purpose-built fortress in the middle of central Lahore, the Academy was one of the many things the British forgot to pack up with them when they left the Indian subcontinent in 1947. As far as anyone can tell, the Victorian-era institution's main goal was to colonize South Asian children to serve in nineteenth-century British colonial bureaucracies, though many people also speak fondly of the kebabs.

"Our family has been going here for generations," my father said as he tied my shoelaces on my first day of school. Dad was always the one who got me ready in the morning, packed me a sandwich for lunch, and made sure that my morning tea wasn't too scalding. "They survived, didn't they?" he said with a comforting smile.

"Granddad died of a heart attack before I was born," I reminded him.

"Yes," he replied. "Well . . ."

He drove me to school, as he would do every day for the next decade, and walked me to my classroom door, where he knelt down and kissed my cheek. "I love you," he said, his eyes slightly teary. "Be good." I spent that first day in petrified silence, desperate to hide the fact that I didn't speak a word of Urdu, Pakistan's national language, in a classroom full of children who spoke little else. The Academy grounds resembled a venerable college campus more than a children's school. The high school classes were held in the older buildings—nineteenth-century domed structures lined with arched balconies and sumptuously decorated in slabs of veined marble and carved limestone—while the middle and primary schools were in the relatively new brick buildings across campus, though these too had domes. Towering trees flanked the dozens of paved roads and dirt paths that crisscrossed the beautifully manicured school grounds. Inside the fortified boundary walls of the Academy was everything needed to run what amounted to a small town: Aside from a plethora of administrative buildings, the campus boasted hockey fields, cricket pitches, squash courts, swimming pools, football fields, rose gardens, hospitals, mosques, tailors, grocery stores, cobblers, dormitories, teachers' bungalows, libraries, stables, aviaries, and even an amphitheater. Most of the classrooms were large and bright, with built-in wooden shelving already smoothed by the touch of thousands of inmates by the time I arrived. The ceilings were unusually tall, well over forty feet, and lined at the top with slits of narrow windows, an old South Asian architectural trick to let warm air escape that was just effective enough that the school never invested in air-conditioning despite the hundred-degree Punjabi summers.

The regal beauty of my new surroundings did nothing to temper the school's pervasive culture of brute aggression. Our English public school uniforms were meant to obscure any economic difference between the students, but it didn't take long for me to become impatient with the prickly collars (who wears a cravat before seven A.M., who?) and the daily inspections into the state of my hair or shoes, violations for which children as young as six were routinely beaten with bamboo canes. I could already tell there was no show-and-tell here, no chocolate milk, not even the suggestion of a nap. In the first half hour of class, the boy in front of me took a poo on his seat and began wailing.

"Are you English?" one of the other kids asked me during recess as we examined the turd later. He was intrigued that I couldn't speak Urdu, a by-product I now trace to the severe Anglicization of both sides of my family and a personal dedication to Julie Andrews's filmography.

"I don't know," I replied, in what I still think is rather prophetic postcolonial self-awareness, but he beat me up anyway. When I reached home I begged my parents to take me back to the naps of the American School, but they refused.

"But they hit children there!" I yelled, dimly aware that this was just the beginning of much longer prison sentence. "And there is poo!" I added. "Everywhere!"

"You'll learn to like it," they said. "Give it time," they said. My mother saw my crushed face and touched my cheek gently. "It'll get better," she whispered.

"How do you know?" I asked though the tears.

She smiled and reached for her well-worn tarot deck, quickly shuffling the cards and laying them out in the shape of a cross. "See?" she said, triumphantly holding up a card with an overflowing chalice on it. "The ace of cups! That means you'll have a wonderful time!"

"Can't argue with the tarot!" my father said. To appease me, they added that one of my favorite cartoons, *The Jungle Book*, was set in Lahore, and wasn't it wonderful that I now got to live in the same place as Mowgli? But the veiled threat of infant homelessness did little to improve my mood. Besides, I reasoned, the Lahore I saw around me—with its choked roads, open sewers, and crowded concrete shopping arcades—looked nothing like the lush jungles in the cartoon.

Forced to reconcile my glittering inner life with this rancid new reality, I took a full month to stop crying at the prospect of school every morning. Things didn't improve much until I met Zariyan.

My family and I moved into a tiny semidetached redbrick town house nestled in a large, leafy neighborhood that was otherwise entirely overgrown with sprawling colonial-era homes. The proximity to VIP housing meant there was lots of ambient security but very little traffic in the streets. Being the youngest kid by a decade is quite like being an only child, and I took advantage of my independence by stalking the alleys around the house fairly unsupervised. Eventually a group of neighborhood children began including me in their daily cricket games. Their parents worked as cooks and drivers in the surrounding houses—distinctions that are allowed to mean nothing at that age—and I was grateful for their friendship. They all spoke a rapid-fire mix of Punjabi and Urdu, and through them I began to pick up bits and pieces of the languages (or "vernacular," as my very colonized grandmother used to say between sips of Earl Grey tea). Months passed until one day an unfamiliar face with a decidedly American accent joined our afternoon cricket matches. (Before you ask, cricket was as indecipherable a game to me then as it is now. The truth is I didn't play so much as lie in glorious repose on a tree branch channeling Bob Fosse while waiting for the captain to take his shirt off.)

Zariyan was skinny, friendly, and, despite our three-year age difference (I was six, he was nine), about my height. He too was enrolled
at the Academy, a few years ahead of me, and it turned out he lived
close to my house. He invited me over for a game of catch and we
quickly bonded over our shared love of sketching and the American
daytime soap opera *Santa Barbara*. That I now had a neighborhood
friend I could visit without asking an adult to drive me over made
me feel wildly independent, just like the kids on *The Wonder Years*.
Zariyan had also moved to Pakistan from abroad, but unlike me, he
didn't need picture albums to remember his life there. We spent the
long, hot afternoons of our first summer together inventing games
under his grandmother's knotted mango tree while he regaled me with
fairy tales of American shopping malls, indoor fountains, branded
toys, and miles of amusement park rides.

"Is America really as cool as it is on TV?" I asked.

"Better," he assured me.

We became inseparable. Most days I returned from school only to
drop my bag off before heading to his place until well past dinner.
His whole family had quasi-American accents, affectations they
maintained by spending their summers in Indiana, which I was dis-
appointed to learn wasn't a colony for Indians on holiday. Zariyan
returned from his summer vacation in 1992 utterly obsessed with
Disney's *Aladdin*. He had the action figures, the bedsheets, the video
game, and even a plastic model of the magical cave. We watched
the cartoon every single day, excited by the fact that for the first
time the animated world on our TV looked somewhat like the one
around us. Lahore too had an old mosque with three giant domes
and an arched palace surrounded by the winding alleys of bustling
bazaars. Even the turbans in the movie felt oppressively familiar.
(One of the Academy's more indigenous rituals was its insistence
that every Friday all students arrive at morning assembly wearing
Punjabi-style turbans, dramatically flamboyant headpieces made

with heavily starched muslin wrapped so that it fanned across our heads like the tail of a mating peacock. They felt quite fabulous, truth be told, but the humidity of Lahore made the show of pomp somewhat impractical, since almost immediately after putting one on, the starched cloth would sag like a wilted petal, so that by nine A.M. it looked like the whole student body was wearing the same wet stripper wig.)

One afternoon, shortly after his arrival back in Lahore, Zariyan and I were in his bedroom singing along to "A Whole New World" when he turned, took my face in both his hands, and kissed me on the lips. He was tentative at first and then, when he saw I didn't object, pressed on with wetter purpose. I felt his tongue circle mine and we burst into embarrassed giggles.

"What was that?" I asked, the metallic taste of him still fresh on my lips.

"It's called kissing," he said. "French kissing."

"What's French about it?"

"The tongue," he said with authority. We resumed watching the cartoon, the rug beneath us both now as weightless as Aladdin's.

I had already known I liked looking at boys before that (swimming pool stalking), but that's when I realized I *liked* boys. Our kisses progressed from tentative to tenacious, our hugs from clothed to shirtless, until eventually our private games required no clothes at all. I had not yet learned to be ashamed of my desire for him, but watching Zariyan check and recheck that the door was locked was my first hint that games like ours weren't strictly halal.

The obvious difference in our bodies fascinated me. Zariyan was ochre-skinned, scrawny, and tightly packed with visible muscle from playing sports every day. I, by comparison, was pink, pudgy, and pen-dulous, doubtless because instead of playing sports I choreographed slow-moving beauty pageant entrance numbers down ornate stair-cases, but we don't always get to choose our talents.

After his dad nearly walked in on us grinding into each other's erections one afternoon, we began using Zariyan's grandfather's empty house next door whenever we wanted to "do that." The house had been abandoned years before, and he was sure no one would find us in the musty mansion of forgotten rooms even if they tried. We were too young to have specific destinations to these physical joinings, no culmination or consummation, just the curiosity of caress.

"I wish there was no one else in the world but us," he said to me afterward one day as we picked warm blackberries off a tree in his back garden.

"That would be sad," I said, thinking of a world without my parents in it.

"Not if we had each other," he said. "We could live together all alone, and play together whenever we wanted." He blushed despite his obvious hard-on. "We could draw and paint and watch movies and no one would bother us ever, ever, ever! For the rest of our lives if . . . if we wanted."

The heated pleasure of our games had been gradually tempered by an ice-cold fear of discovery. I realized quickly that, much like when I played with Barbies, it was somehow wrong of me to feel this whole. My joy had to be hidden behind locks and secrets and guilt. Even then I was slightly embarrassed that my stomach jiggled when I moved, but Zariyan never made fun of me for my weight, and when I was naked with him I felt like the luckiest kid in the world. I imagined us as a couple, spending blissful schoolless days drawing pictures and watching cartoons, never once scared of who would walk in on us and never once afraid of what would happen if they did. At night I'd snuggle into his arms and we'd laugh at the latest episode of *The Simpsons*. Wouldn't it be loverly?

"Yes," I said. "Yes, that does sound nice."

The wail of the sunset azaan pierced the evening birdsong.

"I have to go do homework." He leaned to kiss me. "See you tomorrow?"

We were nine and twelve now, comfortable enough in our practiced routine to begin taking risks. One day after lunch, Zariyan and I went into my room to get naked, one of the few times I remember being more excited than guilt-ridden at what we were about to do. Our sweaty bodies were completely intertwined on my squeaky twin bed when suddenly the door to the room burst open. My middle sister stood framed in the doorway, her mouth frozen in a silent O.

"Wha—" she began, but Zariyan grabbed my hand and together we fled into the bathroom, naked, panting, and red-faced.

"Shit!" he said, bolting the door shut behind us. "Shit! Shit! Shit!"

A knock. We froze.

He raised a trembling finger. *Stay quiet.*

Another knock, angrier.

"I know you're in there!"

"Y-yes?" I replied.

"Is Zariyan in there with you?" my sister demanded.

We remained quiet and eventually she left. Some moments later there was another knock, softer. Mother.

"Komail." She was trying hard to sound kind. "Will you come out of there?"

"In a minute," I replied, somewhat hysterically.

When we finally heard retreating footsteps, I told Zariyan to walk out with me, but he was on the floor rocking back and forth, his red swollen eyes fixed on the blue flowers on the bathroom tiles.

"They know," he muttered, fat tears streaming down the hollows of his cheeks. "They all know now. Everyone . . ."

"It's OK," I found myself lying. "It'll be fine. Take my hand. I promise, it'll be fine." We gingerly stepped out to find that our clothes still lay in an undisturbed crumpled line from door to bed. We dressed while avoiding each other's gaze—an early lesson that eye contact is often more intimate to gay men than nudity—and after making sure the coast was clear, I helped him sneak out the back door so no one would see him.

They all know now, I thought as I watched him jump over the brick wall to his home. *Everyone will*. It was a shame that my middle sister was the one who caught us. She was by far the most religious member of my family.

"You have to pray for me," she'd often instruct me as a child.

"Why?"

"God listens to the prayers of children. Children are without sin."

My sister's assumption that I was a pure child made me feel instantly dirty even then because, to paraphrase Britney, I wasn't that innocent. One day they'd know why and so would God. Years later, when I was fifteen, it was she who would force me to swear on a holy book that I wasn't gay and never would be. That I was usually asked to pray to God that she find a great man to marry while she insisted I never do the same is the kind of irony it takes years of therapy to find amusing.

Once Zariyan left, my mother summoned me into the pink expanse of her perfumed bedroom. She sat perched on the edge of her bed watching me as I entered, and told me to lock the door behind me. I was trembling.

"Little children," she began, staring up at the ceiling fan in search of words she never wanted to find.

"I'm sorry," I cried, flinging myself toward the comfort of her chest. "I'm so sorry! It won't happen again!"

"Promise." There was relief in her voice but her arms remained stiff by her side. "Promise me that you'll never do it again."

"I p-promise."

"Good," she said and wiped the tears from my cheeks. To see her face soften felt like love. "It's very . . ." She stopped herself.

"Very what?"

"Dangerous," she finished. *Dangerous.*

"Please," I begged her. "Don't tell Dad."

She looked at me for a long moment and then nodded.

"I won't."

Zariyan waited for my mother to tell his about what had happened, but after a nerve-wracking month passed without incident, I persuaded him that it was finally safe to visit me again. He came over with a coloring book, which was odd because he'd always said he was too old for them. As we sat at the dining table with a box of crayons and performed our juvenile innocence for the adults, I resisted the urge to feel the warmth of a body as familiar to me as my own. He left after three pages and a few knowing glances between my mother and sister.

Eventually we settled into a supervised routine of Sega Mega Drive, comic books, and Monopoly—anything appropriately childlike and non-nude. It took me six months to work up the courage to ask my mother if I could go to Zariyan's house to play unsupervised.

"You're not going to be up to your old *tricks* again, are you?" she asked, her thin eyebrow arched precariously high.

"No," I said, staring at the dirt.

And I left my first few meetings with Zariyan genuinely proud of myself for having resisted the temptation to touch him, despite his own insistence. But one day I relented, and walked home that night feeling weak, confused, and miserable at my own inability to defeat whatever demon it was inside me that made me this way. I was, even then, acutely aware that this was no regular childish transgression washed away by the scrub of an apology. It wasn't like when I broke the drawing room window doing my Vivien Leigh impression or tried to push my grandmother down a flight of stairs during a trip to the Hanging Gardens of Babylon in Iraq. I hadn't simply done something wrong; it felt that I—the very essence of me—*was* wrong.

Riddled with a tapeworm of guilt, that evening I ate two cheese toasts, which made me feel surprisingly better. So I ate another two, and then two more. Eating was how my family processed emotions, so no one really noticed when I finished an entire cake by myself. Within three months I went from being a slightly pudgy aesthete to winning "Fattest Boy in School" at the Academy, a category I would go on to dominate for several years until a boy from Qatar with breathtaking thyroid issues joined us in the ninth grade.

My body fat became the locus of my external identity, the first thing people noticed about me and the last thing they remembered. But the prize did come with an all-you-can-eat gift certificate to Pizza Hut, so, you know, small victories.

Chapter 2

A COCK, IN A FROCK,
ON A ROCK

BY 1994, PULSE GLOBAL CASSETTE tapes revolutionized the (admittedly niche) Pakistani home entertainment market overnight. Radiating brand-name authenticity, the sleek VHS tapes were a welcome change from the horrors dubbed "camera prints" one had had to endure in the country until then, shaky bootleg copies of Western films recorded on handheld cameras in dark foreign movie theaters. The only advantage to camera prints was that, in a world well before streaming, you got to see Hollywood movies within days of their theatrical release rather than five months later. The major downside, as I discovered with *Jurassic Park*, is that you can miss all the best bits if someone in the front row wears a wide-brimmed hat. The Urdu subtitles sometimes made up for the dismal quality, though, perhaps best illustrated with *Jurassic Park*'s pivotal T-Rex chase, where the actors' terrified screams were translated as "Run! Run! The fat lizard is coming!"

But 1994's true breakout hit was about dragons of an altogether different variety: *The Adventures of Priscilla, Queen of the Desert,* an Australian indie movie about three drag queens on a cross-country road trip of sequined self-discovery. The film had all the usual elements—queer self-deprecation, off-camera sex scenes, the adulation of heteronormative family structures—that allowed straight people to watch gay stories without spontaneously combusting into fiery judgment. At the end, when a young Hugo Weaving comes to grips with his newly discovered role as a father, there was probably a truck driver in Somewhere, Wisconsin, thinking, *Well*, shit, *they're just like us.*

Some of us, I thought, sizzling with envy at the satin opera gloves the queens wore for their climactic hike up Uluru.

I was not entirely unfamiliar with drag (quelle surprise), starting with British Christmas pantomimes that routinely cast men in the female parts. But the sparkling creatures on English language TV looked very different to the hijras (or *khwaja siras*) I often saw begging on the streets at traffic lights in Lahore. My mother had told me they were "men in women's clothes," but we were taught at school that they constituted a separate third gender, neither boy nor girl and so somehow lesser than both. It would take many years of brave activism on their part for Pakistani law to finally recognize them as a protected class of citizens, able to work, earn wages, and even run for office (the same rights are not afforded to trans men, because misogyny). Some of them may well have been gay men forced to live as women, while others were women trapped in male bodies, but they all were condemned to a life of prejudice and ridicule in a place too closed-minded to recognize the cosmic expanse of their glory.

I remember two *khwaja siras* who used to stand at the traffic light right outside the Academy's main gate, swishing confidently from car to car as they promised to pray for people's good health in exchange for a few rupees. They wore flimsy cotton *dupattas* draped over their heads and their *shalwar kameeze*s were old but well maintained.

I often wondered what their faces looked like under the layers of gray-white foundation and strips of garish eye shadow but felt too ashamed to make actual eye contact when they approached in case anyone suspected I was one of them. School bullies already hissed "*khusra*" under their breath whenever I passed.

Surrounded as I was by overweight raspy smokers at both school and home, I naturally assumed all fabulous women had deep baritones and a quick wit. (My own drag name used to be Komu LaWhore for obvious reasons, but age has whittled that into, well, ladies and gentlemen, please welcome to the stage . . . Aunty Climax. *hope for applause*) Despite the daily terror of the tyrants-in-training at the Academy, the major upshot of being at an all-male institution was that boys had to play the female parts in school plays. I auditioned every year, feigning outrage but secretly delighted to be cast in meaty roles like Beggar Witch, Rich Woman 2, or Angry Stepmother. For Rich Woman 2, the teacher brought in a lovely secondhand pink taffeta ballgown studded with periwinkle blue bows that I accessorized with my mother's silver heels, which I knew from experience were dance appropriate. My family indulged these fancies by reasoning that I was just a young kid playing dress up, and even my mother lent me a pair of gold clip-on earrings for opening night.

It was windy as I strutted toward the school amphitheater in full regalia, the yards of my pink taffeta gown billowing behind me like a gay cloud. It wasn't that I wanted to actually *be* a girl, but rather that the official benediction of this transgression of gender roles meant that, just this once, I had no fear of being visibly different despite my four-foot train. On stage, my obvious effeminacy was no longer a radioactive secret but an explosive asset. In character I was immune to barbs about my growing chest, cocooned from cruelty over my chubby legs, and oblivious to the shame of my sagging stomach. I felt alive, free, and deeply fabulous. That sense of inner peace, when your outer world supports your inner self like an ergonomic lower-back pillow, is what I imagine straight people feel like most of the time.

The play was a triumph, and I curtsied demurely at curtain call to a deafening roar of applause. The next year I auditioned for *Sleeping Beauty* with my eye on the role of the queen, but the director, Mrs. Aziz, told me I'd become too fat over the summer to pass as a girl, no doubt a result of my recent discovery of soft cheeses. Women, she insisted, weren't meant to be large but rather thin and beautiful. I would play the king instead, and no more tears. I stormed off, furious, not least because Mrs. Aziz herself was the size of a tomb. To soothe myself, I came home and rewatched *Priscilla, Queen of the Desert* while inhaling slices of vanilla pound cake slathered in lashings of cold whipped cream.

Priscilla remains decades ahead of its time. Not having to pander to American middle management meant the movie didn't reduce queer men to supporting friends or hospice patients. To recognize the radical authenticity of *Priscilla*, you need only watch its American knockoff, the laboriously titled *To Wong Foo, Thanks for Everything! Julie Newmar*. I can almost picture a Hollywood producer bulging red-faced at a printout of *Priscilla*'s gross profits while screaming at a hapless assistant, "Get me a drag queen road trip movie NOW!"

The assistant came up with Patrick Swayze, Wesley Snipes, and John Leguizamo spending a weekend in perpetual drag courting tolerance in a dust-bowl town with depressing architecture. If *Priscilla* was a diamond tiara, *To Wong Foo* was a cardboard crown. Lazily conceived but wonderfully acted, the running joke of the casting was "look at these manly movie stars wearing dresses," a feat better left to the queer classic *Some Like It Hot*. Personally, if I was driving from New York to LA in 1995, I would not wear a floor-length red ballgown to a highway town, I don't care how many kind housewives lived there. But a disappointing drag queen movie was still a cultural diamond in the dark trenches of the nineties, and I will personally remain forever grateful for RuPaul's cameo, in which she descends on a trapeze wearing a Confederate-flag gown playing a drag queen named—wait for it—Rachel Tensions.

My mother and sisters were obsessed with Patrick Swayze as both dirty dancer and spectral potter, and it probably didn't sit well with them to see their heartthrob lace up a corset and glue on fake lashes, because we only rented the movie once, although I would secretly eye it at the video store for years afterward with a clandestine desire usually reserved for the men's underwear sections at department stores.

The next year, when my family sat down to watch the camp classic *The Birdcage* (also based on a musical), I began to piece together a working theory. Maybe, just maybe, being a boy who liked other boys wasn't dangerous everywhere; maybe it was just dangerous *here*. After all, I reasoned, *Some Like It Hot* was set in 1929, when the world was black and white, and no one minded when Jack Lemmon's character got engaged to another man at the end. In the seventies sitcom *Three's Company*, Jack Tripper routinely pretended to be gay, and even *Friends* had a lesbian wedding. The world must be bipolar. Here and there. "Here" was the hot country of locked doors and dangerous kisses where I lived, a place where my liberal parents hid their wine bottles in sock drawers, where my sisters never wore jeans outside the house, and where someone was always watching you. But "there" was America: a verdant land of abundant acceptance, a faraway sanctuary where gay men could live as loving couples, own businesses, perform in shows, and even raise children together in slightly tacky oceanfront apartments. This plastic illusion of a gay USA had little to do with the brutal reality of the country where Matthew Shepard would soon be tortured and left to die by the side of a country road. But visions of this distant utopia, however unreal, cut through the oppressive fog of the Islamic Republic like shards of light piercing through a thatched roof.

"Are we gay?" I asked Zariyan one day as we lay naked in his bed.

"No," he replied quickly.

"But you didn't even think about it! How do you *know*?"

He put the collector's-edition Batman comic he was reading down on his bare thighs.

"Because," he said. "Gay men have AIDS."

"AIDS." It sounded like a charity gala for teen mothers. "What's that?"

"It's a disease that kills grown-up guys who . . ." He paused.

"Who . . . ?"

"Who, you know, they touch each other," he said furtively.

"Like us?"

"Like us."

"And it *kills* them?"

"Yeah," he said, grinning. "One touch and . . ." He traced a line across his neck with a finger. "Dead."

I went quiet for a long time, long enough that he stopped laughing.

"What's wrong?"

"When are we going to die?" I asked.

He smiled. "We're not grown-ups," he said, rubbing my head. "We'll be OK. It's got nothing to do with us."

"Promise?"

"Promise."

Finding out there was a fatal disease only for gay men felt like obvious confirmation that God hated me. I was both terrified and furious that no one had told me about AIDS sooner. Is this what my mother meant when she said "dangerous"? Did my family already know? Did everybody? The men in *Priscilla* seemed healthy enough, I reasoned, but they also hadn't really touched each other in the movie. Or even kissed, come to think of it.

Shit.

I spent the next five months convinced that any actor who ever played a gay role on-screen was long dead of AIDS. When I saw Robin Williams's first post-*Birdcage* movie at the rental store, I jumped up and down holding the *Patch Adams* cassette screaming, "He's alive! He's alive!" at a bewildered retail assistant.

Obviously no one else at the Academy had seen *Priscilla* (a stark reminder that I was always a bird of paradise in a nest of sparrows), despite the fact that most of my teachers looked like drag queens. Sadly, that's where the resemblance ended and the cruelty began. The Academy felt like it was expressly founded to spread the potent cancer of colonial-era white supremacy, but with no more white people around, its culture appeared to have evolved over the decades into a confusing mash-up of colorism, corporal cruelty, and class conflict. It seemed to proudly uphold the kind of British exceptionalism rooted in overt racism that routinely casts indigenous people everywhere as savages unless they can quote Keats unprovoked. I can see now the invisible strings of class, privilege, access, and education that allowed me to speak English more fluently as a child than most of my teachers, but at the time it upended the delicate power dynamic between us because I knew the meaning of the word "retaliate" but Mrs. Ruby didn't.

Perhaps that's why she was always angry. Short, bulbous, and incurably fond of blue eye shadow, Mrs. Ruby had a widespread reputation for inflicting painful punishments on children for arbitrary reasons, which may have had to do with the rumor that her husband had taken a second wife over the summer break (polygamy is legal in Islam for men, as I discovered later from my high school chemistry lab partner, who had three mothers but no deodorant). Once, in grade five, my whole class failed a pop quiz and Mrs. Ruby screamed at us to form a line in front of her desk. One by one she forced ten-year-olds to walk up to her, fists out, and rapped our tiny knuckles with a razor-edged wooden ruler until she drew blood. When the boy in front of me tried to run away, she grabbed him by his collar, stood on both his feet, and slapped him across the face repeatedly.

"Boys"—*thwap*—"don't"—*thwap*—"cry"—*thwap*—"understand?"

It was my turn next, so I screwed my eyes shut and held out my hand, but nothing happened. I peeked through my wet eyelashes to see her deep red lips curled into a menacing smile.

"*Ufff*," she sighed, gripping my quivering chin in her crimson talons. "Such fair skin! Such long eyelashes! Go back to your seat, sweetheart. Who can hit a face like that?"

I glided back to my desk, radiating smugness. When the boy next in line complained about favoritism, Mrs. Ruby grabbed him by the ear and smashed his face into the chalkboard five times. As I watched him shuffle back to his seat, face hung low to hide the sobs, my smugness gave way to guilt: Why did she hit him and not me? What power had let me off the hook, and how, I wondered for months afterward, can I harness it to protect myself in the future? Not just from the teachers, but from the students who punished me for the same reasons that Mrs. Ruby didn't.

Life at the Academy was like Pakistan itself: arbitrary, changeable, unpredictable, its rules apparently more rooted in colorism and perceived class than any pretense of merit. There would be worse teachers at the Academy than Mrs. Ruby, and harsher punishments too, but she was the first to demonstrate that our world was more complicated than implied by the primary colors of right and wrong. There were invisible forces at work that adjudicated crime and punishment, and if you had enough access, it was possible to skirt punishment altogether. I could be slapped for being effeminate one day but given a kiss for being fair-skinned the next. The Academy, for all its self-aggrandizing speeches on scholastic aptitude and courtly manners, actively taught its children how to weaponize those invisible forces for their own personal advancement and, consequently, gave them the tools to thrive in a corrupt country. George Michael was wrong. In order to survive you gotta have more than faith; you gotta have privilege. And for that early lesson, I would like to start by thanking the Academy . . .

Chapter 3

GURL . . .

EING AN EFFEMINATE BOY IS like carrying a bomb only other people can detonate, and I spent most of my child-hood hiding the trigger switch from casual arsonists. My effeminacy was not subtle. It radiated out from me, unctuous and languid as a bright pink halo, and its unmistakable presence invited a constant stream of corrective criticism from the adults around me. Don't sit like that, don't walk like that, don't move your hands like that, don't cross your legs like that, don't listen to the Spice Girls, don't hang that *Buffy* poster, don't play with dolls, don't re-create the beauty pageant evening gown segment using three bathrobes and your great-grandmother's wedding sari, don't, don't, don't. Gay boys who are unable to hide our gayness from the world are told early and often that there is something inherently wrong with us that needs fixing. But it can't be fixed by our parents or siblings or teachers or bullies (despite their fanatic interest). No, we alone are responsible because we alone are broken. Perhaps this is why so many of us go on to develop wicked tongues and insatiable revenge fantasies. It didn't help that Urdu, like French, is a grammatically gendered language, meaning everything in the world is deemed either feminine or masculine. A woman uses different words than a man, and if you're trying to prove you're actually a boy to demanding classmates, it can all get rather complicated. They called me a sissy whenever I mistakenly used the feminine verb, so I stopped using it at all, which meant they made fun of me for not being Pakistani enough. In my defense, my family spoke English at home, so how in the world was I meant to intuit that "car" in Urdu is feminine but "bed" is masculine? Or that "bridges" are masculine but "guns" are feminine? Even electrical outlets have a gender (feminine). Deathly afraid of physical confrontation, I fought my changing roster of bullies in my own nonviolent way, firing off bitchy quips memorized from daily viewings of *The Bold and the Beautiful*, *Dynasty*, and *Absolutely Fabulous*.

"Your mother should have used a *knitting needle!*" I screamed at a boy as our sixth-grade geography teacher looked on blandly, but it's amazing how ineffective a devastating comeback is against a solid fist.

Middle school meant that I now studied in the same brick building as Zariyan's year, a proximity I'd been anticipating for years. In my daydreams we were as inseparable as the couples I saw every week on *Beverly Hills, 90210*, walking down school corridors holding hands, our recess spent together in deserted locations, conjoined, complete, and content. To say nothing of how cool I'd be when the other kids found out I knew an actual eighth grader.

I spotted him on the first day of term walking across the grassy quadrangle at the center of a pentagram of sporty boys. While we all had the same summer uniform of a white short-sleeved shirt tucked into khaki pants, Zariyan wore his with practiced apathy; hair messy, belt hung low, shirt unbuttoned well past the scar on his sternum he got after falling into barbed wire last summer.

"Hey, Zariyan!" I said, bubbling with excitement as he approached.

A look of panic swept across his face but quickly resolved itself into malice. "Hey bitchtits," Zariyan said. The friends laughed.

"Who's that?" I overheard one of them ask him as they walked on. "No idea," he replied.

He told me later that he hadn't wanted his friends to get the "wrong idea" about us. That I wasn't one of his friends was assumed, but that the idea was only wrong about him was implied. But I took him at his word, and we resumed our after-school friendship under a new layer of shame. Three years is an impressive difference at that age, and I usually deferred to his sense of authority, like when he told me sperm came out in one long noodle like toothpaste, or that the platypus didn't really exist in nature. *He has pubes*, I'd reason, *of course he knows more.*

But Zariyan wasn't just changing physically. The older we grew, the more difficult it had become to maneuver around the minefield of his internalized guilt. I now noticed that our "games" had only ever been on his timetable. If I tried to touch him unsolicited, he would recoil, insisting that I behave like a "normal" kid, while ten minutes later he'd blast the Backstreet Boys on his CD player and start sucking me off. I still tingled when I heard "A Whole New World," but the rug beneath us no longer felt weightless.

In middle school the days went from feral to penal very quickly. All the teachers on this new battlefield were men, and we learned firsthand they did not need wooden rulers to inflict physical pain. I had done poorly in my exams ("careless but confident" ever a running chorus), and so was transferred at half term to a section for academic underachievers, mostly populated by children who used "motherfucker" instead of "please."

Eating still made almost anything feel better, and the consequences showed. My chest sagged, my stomach protruded, and my flanks stretched out in luxurious abandon until, by the year's end, my silhouette looked like the body of a concert-grade cello. I spent my recesses alone, doodling in sketchbooks or else wandering the Academy's many acres while munching on masala potato chips, careful to avoid the crowds of Not-Friends playing cricket in the fields. I prayed daily for gravity to suddenly reverse itself and hurtle me into outer space, safe from the torment of games on earth.

Avoiding sports took up a considerable amount of my time, actually, especially since we were forced to stay after school for two hours (*two* hours) to play a different group activity every day. Cricket, hockey, football, basketball, running, it was always the same trauma: Send three hundred boys into an open field and may the odds be ever in your favor. I stayed away, both because no one had ever taught me how to play any contact sports (why do people assume this information is preloaded into boys at birth? The only thing I knew coming into the world was that I loathe kitten heels) but also because playing cricket with real cricket balls is like dodging a cannonball every two minutes. Whenever forced to participate under the threat of expulsion, I chose positions that promised minimal cardio, civilized roles like goalkeeper or umpire, anything that granted me a punitive air of authority. But one misty afternoon in January I arrived at evening games to find that my sedentary position had been filled.

"By who?!"

The teacher pointed at a slightly plump boy with short black hair sitting by the goalpost reading a thick book, a discarded field-hockey stick next to him on the grass.

"What are you doing here?" I demanded after I stomped over. He looked up at me through thick black-rimmed spectacles that made his eyes look three times larger.

"Hiding," he replied. "Like, *duh*."

I was too surprised that someone else had seen *Clueless* to be offended. "From who?" I asked, and he raised a finger vaguely in the direction of the pubescent east, where a fist fight had broken out over who was going to be captain that day.

"You're not allowed to read books during games, you know," I said, pointing to his leather-bound copy of *Anna Karenina*. "They give you a pink card for that." (That the worst disciplinary punishment one could get at the Academy was a pink card is the kind of symbolism only nonfiction allows.)

"Are you going to tell on me?" he asked. I recognized the icy fear in his voice, but the thought that I could use this opportunity to prove my loyalty to our mutual oppressors evaporated like steam.

"No," I said, dropping my hockey stick down on the grass besides his. "It's just there's a better spot to hide over there. You see? Behind the bamboos?"

He grinned wide, revealing a full set of silver braces that glittered in the afternoon haze. We waited until the teacher was distracted by another brawl before running over to hide in the foliage.

"I'm Komail," I said, descending backward onto the ground like Nosferatu.

"Jibran," he said, extending his hand to me palm down like an empress.

"Are you new here?" I asked.

"Brand new. Just moved here from Islamabad."

"Ah. So, what's your favorite class?"

"Hmm," he said. "Aristocracy."

Fabulous.

"Do you like comic books?" Jibran asked.

"Duh," I said, grinning.

"Oh, *really*? OK then, let's see . . . Dark Phoenix versus Apocalypse?"

A test.

"Dark Phoenix," I replied with a confidence I never felt in math class.

"Reasoning?"

"She ate a whole *star* system before destroying the Shi'ar battleships." Jibran tried to not look impressed, but I could tell he approved. "OK, OK," I said. "My turn! Psylocke versus the White Queen?"

He furrowed his brow. "Psylocke for the weapons," he said slowly. "But Emma Frost for the corset."

Utterly fabulous!

On we went, Cheetarah versus She-Ra, She-Hulk versus the Scarlet Witch, Destiny's Child versus TLC, Margaret Thatcher versus Benazir Bhutto.

"Storm versus Rogue?"

"Storm *is* a goddess," I confirmed.

"Isn't she, though?" Jibran sighed. Just then a volley of screams pierced our calm bubble and we both emerged to see a phalanx of angry boys hurtling down the hockey field running toward us armed with wooden sticks and hormonal rage.

"Defend the goal!" one was shouting, presumably at us. "Defend the goaaaaal!"

I turned, but Jibran had already vanished behind a bush. The shouts grew louder, so I reluctantly ambled out of the thicket, picked up my hockey stick like a wand, and tried to follow the white blur zigzagging toward me like a homing beacon of humiliation. I planted myself squarely in the center of the goalpost, praying that sheer size would stop what hand-eye coordination could never. The attacker locked eyes with me and smirked. *Easy victory*, I heard him think. He pulled the hockey stick back and swung, but there was a flick and suddenly he was pushing air, the white ball already whizzing toward the opposite end of the pitch. The threat retreated.

"That was close," Jibran said, emerging from the bushes with a yellow flower tucked behind his ear. "Now then, where were we?"

"Storm versus Rogue," I said, throwing the hockey stick down again.

We became best friends quickly and the ranking game became our morning ritual, like how my straight cousins talked about Ferraris and bikini models. The game always ended, as all such rankings do, with Michelle Pfeiffer's Catwoman, the pleather patron saint of all humans, gay and straight alike.

Jibran owned tapes of the X-Men animated series (still better than any of the movies) and we spent long days worshiping the African weather witch Storm in all her expatriate glory. Our fascination with her explains but does not excuse running around for most of the late nineties shouting, "We are being overwhelmed!" in vaguely foreign accents. In fairness, our veneration wasn't reserved solely for women in Western shows, but rather included any powerful female archetype that embodied our specific sense of subjugated grandeur: Benazir Bhutto, Noor Jehan, Rekha, Sridevi, Nazia Hassan, Angélique Kidjo, Googoosh, Lola Flores, Ofra Haza, even my great-aunt *khala* Boob, with whom Jibran became briefly but entirely obsessed after she made a dramatic entrance to my grandmother's funeral on a wheelchair carried aloft by four straining attendants as she beamed down at the mass of mourners from her lofty perch like a geriatric Cleopatra.

Jibran loved food as much as I did, and between us we could polish off a large pizza in under a minute. Faster with the promise of cake afterward. The consequence of this became increasingly obvious on my chest, which yawned and stretched its way into ever more confident cleavage until even the boys at school begun to take lewd notice.

"Look at those tits, *yaar* . . ."

"They look so *real*."

"Please? Can I touch one? Just one?"

Swimming lessons were hell. We were all assigned the same skimpy swimming trunks, a spandex monstrosity that made my torso look like a water balloon fighting off a tight rubber band. Walking along the outdoor pool in front of the whole student body, my hands folded across my chest for discretion and support, it was impossible for me not to feel a deep sense of physical betrayal in my body. *It's bad enough I act like a girl*, I would scold God during our nightly talks, *did you really have to give me a C cup too?*

To avoid the humiliation of shirtlessness, I'd purposefully loiter in the damp changing rooms until it was too late to join the lesson, or pretend to have forgotten my swimsuit altogether. If all else failed I'd dip my foot in the shallow end before retreating behind the folds of a voluminous bath robe until class ended. All around me skinny boys with no body fat shrugged off their clothes easily, flaunting their bodies to each other with a pride new even to them.

It shouldn't shock you that most women in Pakistan don't wear bikinis while swimming. I've seen a lady wearing a full niqab—Afghan-style—nose-dive into the ocean like a Dementor chasing Harry Potter into the waves. But it may surprise you to learn that it's dispiritingly rare to see shirtless men anywhere either. Religion and other toxic power structures have left Pakistanis with a cavernously deep insecurity about the human body in any form at all. The only reliable exception to this aversion is the Lahore Canal during summertime. The Canal is an irrigation tributary that runs through the center of the city and beyond. Its muddy banks are lined with weeping willows and are flanked on either side by a highway perpetually clogged with commuter traffic. Starting in April, hundreds of men throng to its murky, ice-cold water for relief from the scorching heat. During the hottest months there are so many bodies crammed in the water that from a distance it looks like a blur of thrashing fish. The Canal bathers remained for most of my childhood the only public displays of the unclothed male body I could see, and I was always grateful for the noisy traffic jams that let me gawk at the men on my way home from school every day.

Despite being late September, the summer heat hadn't yet given way to the haze of autumn, and by one o'clock there were already dozens of men in the water, jumping, paddling, laughing, pushing one another off the grassy banks or dragging each other underwater. Most of them wore undershirts even while swimming, but a few did strut around bare-chested, their wet, dark torsos sparkling in the afternoon sun.

A young man walked right by my car, the glimpse of his bare torso awakening me from my daydreams. He looked like a man to me back then, though he was probably no more than seventeen. Still dripping water from his swim, his drooping *shalwar* clung transparently to the expanse of his muscled legs, and I watched furtively as he reached down among the crevices to tug at his dick absentmindedly. I could make out its round, smooth ridges through the wet cloth as clearly as if he had been wearing nothing at all and tried my best to appear nonchalant as I studied what, aside from Zariyan's, was the first penis I'd seen in real life.

His hand ran over the ridges of his flat stomach as he shouted instructions at someone below in Punjabi. I sneezed loudly and, startled, he turned to look back, both he and his penis no more than an arm's length from my open window. I blushed a deep purple and pretended to be fascinated with treetops in the far distance, my heart beating so hard I was certain my mother could hear it from the front seat. But he didn't see me, and after a moment he turned back to climb onto the concrete railing of the bridge, spread his arms, droplets falling off his biceps like diamonds, and jumped into the frigid water below feetfirst.

Jibran taught me all sorts of useful life hacks, like that action figures were a good substitute for the scrutinized child who isn't allowed to buy dolls or that glitter was acceptable in geometric renderings of the Pythagorean theorem. I still saw Zariyan occasionally after school, but his home life had changed dramatically over the last year. His older sister, once a fashionable valedictorian with a panache for winged eyeliner, had recently taken to wearing a black hijab and quoting religious scripture; calligraphic prints of holy verses appeared suddenly at strategic intervals around the house, prayer mats in the corners of rooms, rosaries on the bedside tables; his parents had even hired a bearded cleric to instruct him in the Quran every day after school. Zariyan would tell me about the things he was learning in the lessons—stories of demons, jinns, magic horses, and talking fires—and I enjoyed seeing him reenact the tales, which even then felt like fantasy book plotlines.

"Is that really true?" I asked after he insisted the holy book contained stories of a pair of interdimensional beings who spent their lives licking their way through a magical barrier between our worlds.

"Yup," he said confidently. "Read it myself."

"What, erm, what *else* does it say?"

He knew what I meant.

"It says . . . it's OK for us to, well, *you know* . . ." I feigned ignorance. "We won't go to hell," he said finally, "as long as our dicks don't actually touch skin to skin."

"How would that work?" I said, thinking of the mechanics.

"We'll just wear our underwear, won't we?" He grinned.

Disappointing but logical. Can't be a sin of the flesh if the flesh doesn't touch. It was a relief to know there was a rule book for this somewhere. A familiar heat began to grow inside me, but I knew that Zariyan's information was only ever as reliable as his hormones. Tired of relying on secondhand information and jealous of his singular access to the Divine, I arrived one afternoon at his house during his religious lessons. He didn't like the surprise at all and hissed at me at the door to leave, but the cleric, smelling a new potential client, insisted I join them. The three of us sat down at the dining table, where twin copies of a gilt-edged book were splayed open on identical pages.

The lesson consisted of the cleric reciting verses in guttural Arabic as he swayed back and forth, which Zariyan would then mimic verbatim, sway for sway. I waited for a translation in either Urdu or English, but it seemed that just saying the words in Arabic was enough to be holy. On they went, echoing line after line until the clock in the hall struck five and the cleric closed the book with a reverential kiss on its ornate leather cover.

"Any questions?" he asked.

"No," Zariyan said, already pushing his chair back.

"I have one," I said, my heart pounding. Zariyan glared at me. "What happens to men who love men?" I'd used "love" deliberately. The maulvi, a plump bearded man with kind eyes and yellowing teeth, smiled as I ignored Zariyan's forceful kicks under the table.

The maulvi looked from one of us to the other. "It is natural," he began slowly. "For men to show great affection toward each other. Even love. But if a man touches another man in a way God does not like, well then . . ." He paused.

"Then . . . ?" Zariyan asked, despite himself.

"Then," the maulvi replied cheerfully, "he will be thrown off the highest building in the land to die. If he survives the fall, he is to be bound in rope and stoned."

"To death?" I asked, as if there was less lethal option involving two pebbles and a condom.

"To death," the maulvi confirmed.

We played *Mortal Kombat* 2 after the lesson, sitting as far away from each other as the sofa would allow. I later learned there are as many punishments for sodomy in religious circles as there are practitioners. And although the draconian laws against sodomy were actually inherited from the English colonizers and rarely enforced in Pakistan, I still cannot walk by a tall building without calculating if I'd survive the fall.

Manhattan was pretty triggering my first week.

Most of the trauma of my early years came from the internalization of a larger, punitive religiosity that was floating all around me. God was everywhere in Pakistan, a communal great uncle–meets–town sheriff that the whole country shared. He was in daily greetings, in angry curses, in whispered hopes, in desperate prayers. His name appeared in law books and on currency notes, above war manifestos and below economic treaties. He controlled how time itself was ordered, decided when people took breaks or when school holidays were arranged, how people planned life and livelihoods. Everything from sipping a glass of water to announcing the national debt plan demanded we check in with him at least twice.

But in my home, God felt like a more fluid concept, a comforting if abstract power that had little to do with the rule book of etiquette that every Pakistani around me seemed to know by heart. We were taught in the second grade, for instance, that if a child hasn't learned his five daily prayers in Arabic by his seventh birthday, he is to be turned out onto the streets as punishment for his ingratitude. So convinced was I of my impending eviction that I bawled continuously throughout my seventh birthday party, waiting to be driven to the Canal and abandoned on the pavement like a stray cat. When eventually I stuttered to my parents why I was so upset, they laughed and drew me into a comforting hug. That's nonsense, they said, of course God doesn't want us to kick you out. Here, have some cake.

But if that was nonsense, I wondered, which was the truth? Did this mean I didn't have to sit down every time I drank a glass of water, as Mrs. Ruby insisted? Was God truly angry at kids who didn't play squash, like my PE teacher said? Was heaven really a place without social climbers, as *khala* Boob claimed? I would crash up against this invisible divide between public morality and private faith many more times in my life. Morality in the Islamic Republic of Pakistan is fundamentally elastic, but the heat does that to most things there.

I made sure to keep Zariyan and Jibran separate entities in my life, probably because I subconsciously wanted to protect Jibran from what I knew Zariyan was quickly becoming. The speed of his mood swings had become nauseating. I was too young, too naive to link them to the bruises on his arms, to his bloody lip and his blackened eye.

"Fight at school," he'd say when I noticed a new mark on his face, angrily brushing off any further questions, and I didn't think to ask why his bruises only ever appeared on the weekends his grandfather was around. We still messed around occasionally, but the act felt laden now, the guilt as real as the sweat dripping down our backs. One day in the middle of our bare grindings I felt an unfamiliar wetness spread across my stomach and barely had time to react before he fled into the bathroom and locked the door. I turned on the single overhead bulb to find a thick white fluid smeared across my stomach. I had no clue what it was, so I waited, but when he still hadn't come out after half an hour, I cleaned myself up using the crumpled bedspread and walked home alone. The next day Zariyan called me on the landline.

"We can't hang out anymore," he said.

"Why?"

"Because."

"Because what?

He paused. "Because it's dangerous."

The word sliced right through me.

"You're only three years older than me," I reminded him. "You don't know everything!" *Why was I crying?*

I tried to reason with him, but he hung up. I called back but he didn't pick up, that day or any other. It's strange the kinds of things one remembers. There are entire years in my twenties that are nothing but a blur of smoke and hunger, but I can still trace his old phone number on any keypad.

After what must have been months of hopeful stalking, I finally spotted Zariyan one day at the school parking lot waiting for his car. He was, as usual, surrounded by a group of popular boys. I was with Jibran, which gave me some measure of confidence to say hello as we passed. They looked at us as if the pavement had asked for directions.

"Can we talk?" I said to Zariyan, deliberately ignoring the silent plea in his eyes for me to keep walking, to keep quiet, to keep secrets.

"You know this kid?" the tallest boy asked.

Zariyan looked at the boy and then at me.

"Who?" he replied with a snort. "This *khusra*?"

The friend grinned. *Khusra*, the Urdu word for a transgender woman, is the lowest insult a bully at an all-boys school could summon.

"Khusra," the tall boy repeated. "Khusra!" Kids around us quickly picked up the chant.

"Khusra! Khusra! Khusra!"

Soon it was all I could hear. Eyes began to stare, teachers, students, parents. No one intervened, but for once I didn't care. *If he would only look at me*, I thought. *Please. Please?* But he didn't, and I glared at his eyelids even as I felt Jibran's firm grip dragging me to the opposite end of the parking lot. He led us to our usual secluded spot to wait, and said nothing as the tears dripped down my shuddering cheeks. Jibran's car arrived before mine, but he remained sitting next to me for the next twenty minutes in a compassionate silence for which I've always been grateful.

Chapter 4

YOU'RE JUST A VIRGIN
WHO CAN'T DRIVE

"AVE YOUR BALLS DROPPED YET?" *khala* Boob asked me shortly after my thirteenth birthday.

"No," I replied. "Yours?"

I escaped immediate punishment because my parents were too busy preparing for our flight to America the next morning, and by the time we returned two months later, I found *khala* Boob had done me a solid and died.

It was my first trip to the United States. My parents had means enough that we'd spent some summers in England when I was a child, but foreign vacations were still a very rare treat. Most summer holidays were spent in fits of exploratory patriotism traversing Pakistan's northern mountains, since both my parents believed the only way to truly see one's own country was to put five people in one car for two weeks and see who cracked first.

Despite my bubbling excitement at finally visiting the center of the world as I knew it, I spent most of the eighteen-hour flight from Lahore to Washington, DC, brainstorming strategies to avoid being shirtless on a crowded beach. Thankfully, DC looked nothing like a *Baywatch* episode (geography was never my strength; in college I asked a student from Saskatchewan if he'd voted for Putin). Our first meal was at a local Taco Bell, which naturally meant my next three were spent screaming "Why me?" directly into a toilet bowl. Despite this ignoble start, America more than lived up to her grand reputation. Washington, DC, was the civic embodiment of American imperialist aspirations, a white marble mausoleum built to announce the city as the New Rome of the world's latest powerful empire. Little can prepare first-time visitors for the sheer scale of the United States, evident not just in the waistlines of its citizens but also in the size of the buildings, ice cubes, hot dogs, cars, highways, billboards, and food servings, which probably explain the waistlines. Trips to the grocery store were my favorite thing because, unlike at home, no one in the United States waited for the butcher to decapitate a thrashing chicken or meander through a jungle of hanging goat carcasses. There were no misshapen eggplants here or spotty spinach leaves, no anorexic apples or pockmarked pears. Every fully stocked shelf was a fluorescent-lit altar to capitalist abundance, anointed with powerful totems like Frosted Flakes cereal and Bart Simpson lunch boxes (which lasted exactly nine minutes at school before Abdul Mian stole it at the beginning of term; I know it was you, you little shit). Everything in America looked shiny, plastic, and utterly perfect.

I wept the first time I walked into Costco.

Most of that summer I spent at the Discovery Channel Store, which, next to a Brookstone, was the best place in the mall a kid in the late nineties could waste a few hours unattended. One day, distracted by the fake moon rocks, embalmed insects, and glowing gas lamps, I made the singular mistake of walking onto a machine that promised to reveal which animal in nature you'd be according to weight. The bored assistant lazily snapped a photo and told me to stand on the raised platform in front of a staring crowd. After an expectant pause and the entirely unnecessary sound effect of groaning metal, a sooth-ing female voice boomed over the store's speaker system.

"You," she said in tones of medicated calm, "are two hundred and five pounds, the equivalent of a juvenile humpback whale!" A wall-size screen lit up directly behind me showing my face on the body of whale swimming away from the numbers 205 like they were a Japanese fishing vessel. I assume the machine's illegal now. On the way home I went into a Filene's Basement changing room and stood naked in front of the 180-degree mirror to punish myself. My weight, like my gayness, felt as conspicuous as it did uncontrollable.

We were staying in an area called Dupont Circle, which, depending on who you ask, is a gay hub or politicians' row, and, on the right night, both. I was just excited to be somewhere pedestrians were more than target practice and a curious thirteen-year-old could explore on his own. My daily walks took me near a small bar called the Fireplace, which sounded both cozy and dangerous. There was usually a group of men outside the entrance as I walked by, smok-ing and chatting beneath a rainbow banner that read HAPPY HOUR! MTV had already taught me that the rainbow flag meant "gay," so I spied on the patrons from a Starbucks across the street, imagining what kind of lives they led: Where did they live? What jobs did they have? What really happened inside the dark corners of the Fireplace?

That first encounter with a queer space left me with the mistaken impression that "happy hour" always meant a gay-only hangout, a misunderstanding that would later lead to nasty argument with a Welsh rugby player in Phuket. But simply seeing a gay space from a distance was enough then, because at least it confirmed that they—that we—existed in the real world. It wasn't all just straight actors pretending in movies and tortured subtext in Evelyn Waugh novels. There were real, breathing queer men in the world, and they looked great! (Not coincidentally, that was also the summer I discovered masturbation, and I'd like to take this opportunity to publicly thank the advertising departments of *Men's Health* magazine and Calvin Klein underwear. You did the Lord's work.)

When I returned to Lahore in the fall for my dreaded first year of high school, puberty was already tearing its way through my class like a virus I just couldn't catch. In the space of one summer the utterly unremarkable faces of classmates had transformed into vastly more chiseled offerings. Necks began to bulge and bulges began to drop; puppy fat receded to reveal a jagged landscape of sharp cheekbones and square jaws; scrawny arms grew thick, flat chests puffed wide, and puny shoulders broadened overnight. Not everyone became a male model, mind you—Basit Ali's resemblance to a tampon was so strong it's still his nickname to this day—but everyone appeared to be changing for the better. Except, predictably, me.

While Jibran and I had both turned fugue-state eating into an Olympic sport, I was maddeningly jealous that his fat dispersed itself democratically all over his body whereas mine conspired to pool in dictatorial clumps around my nipples and hips. At thirteen, I looked more like the statue of a pagan fertility goddess than a pubescent boy. Kids would slap my chest in the noisy corridors between class ("Moon-tits!") and teachers would poke at my sagging breasts during class to ask why I didn't play more sports. My boobs were so large that even airport security guards forced me into the women section for my pat down because they didn't believe I was a boy at all. When I told people about my Botticelli-like proportions decades later, they often scoffed in disbelief (lovely feeling), until I confirmed the relief one feels by slicking the sweat away from under a heavy boob fold on a hot summer's day, which is often when women of a certain cup size nodded knowingly.

The rest of me wasn't faring much better. Short and squat, I had rash-ridden red cheeks framed by thick unruly eyebrows determined to stay in constant touch; my love handles had expanded into ebullient C-shaped tragedies, and my stomach protruded outward in pert concentric bulges before eventually slumping over my straining belt buckle in a defeated marsupial flap. The slight dent of my collarbones was the only real proof to me that I had a skeleton at all. The only bit of puberty my body did embrace with singular ambition was cystic acne.

Our academic instruction was still mostly an unimaginative mix of mathematical equations, *To Kill a Mockingbird*, Islamic studies, and revisionist South Asian history. But it seemed clear that there was a concurrent curriculum being silently imparted in high school, one crueler and altogether more important: How to Be a Man. I would have given anything to wake up with the body of the fit teenage boys I saw on television and around me. I prayed every morning for a dust cloud to envelope me after chemistry and transform me in an instant from this depressed fat aesthete with a proclivity for dairy into a terrifying prince with perfect teeth and visible hip bones, but the cloud never came, and I stayed trapped in the confines of a body I detested.

Doesn't matter, I reminded myself between nightly helpings of chocolate fudge brownie and caramel ice cream, *nobody wants to touch you anyway*. My body felt like a treacherous betrayal—I moved like a girl, jerked off to boys, but was desirable to neither. There was some measure of comfort in the thought that at least being fat precluded me from having to display any kind of overt sexuality at school, which I thought helped keep my gay secret, or at the very least avoided confirming it to a hostile mob. After all, no one cared which Bollywood actress I fancied or demanded I tell them how many times I jerked off to the nude scene from *Titanic*. In any case, in the dark ages of the early dial-up internet, most of my jerk-off time was spent less masturbating than masturwaiting for that one paparazzi picture of a naked sunbathing Brad Pitt to load pixel by sun-kissed pixel before someone else in the house picked up the landline and ruined my orgasm.

The white muscular bodies of nineties gay porn models confirmed how different I actually looked from "hot people." I didn't need to shave yet, a mortifying failure at a time when facial hair is the barometer of hormonal high school achievement. Adult masculinity, for so long a distant if inevitable destination at an all-boys school, was so tantalizingly close now that we could smell its musty odor. As high school freshman we shared corridors with upperclassmen, comparative giants who swaggered around with full beards and, if they'd failed to graduate enough times, bald heads. Eager to cast off their childhoods, my classmates began to ape this aura of machismo, strutting around campus with their chins up and chests out, eager to show off the dusting of lip fuzz that had finally joined their three pubes. The very coolest among us had already begun to shave, proudly displaying spotty faces riddled with razor cuts and drenched in acid waves of CK One, the ubiquitous perfume that made a nice change from the scent of oppression and BO that usually wafted down the hallways.

Hormones made the boys more hostile than ever, and to survive the now daily homophobic assaults on us both, Jibran and I constructed a secret syntax with each other, a dialect close to if Greta Garbo and Yoda had a love child that they had raised in isolation at a Ghanaian country club. We transported ourselves away into a comforting world of televised beauty pageants and midcareer Cher albums, anywhere that wasn't the prison yard we were forced into every morning. On the weekends I wasn't stamp collecting with my dad or painting with my mom, we'd lock ourselves away in a room to gorge on camp movies and 12,000 calories of sugar, ready to emerge with entirely new personalities by Monday. Jibran preferred twelve-hour Turner Classic Movies marathons and usually committed to playing variations of a suicidal World War II widow forced to spy for the Germans to save her paraplegic husband from impending execution. I went for *Evita* or, if one had the time, *Yentl*. During recess we'd both stand on the second-story school balcony overlooking the hockey fields, our hands held up high like Madonna as we harmonized: "Don't cry for me, dear Academy, the truth is I never loved you!"

My parents were proud of my artistic talent, otherwise they wouldn't have sent me to summer drawing lessons or bought me sketch pads. But what I also remember is that my love of drawing was usually blamed for my spectacularly bad math reports. Art, absolutely everyone agreed, was not a viable career option for a boy. How will you earn money with drawings? How will you support a family? Where do you think this will lead to in the real world? No, it doesn't matter that you're thirteen, tell us how you'll support your kids, dammit! In those moments, it helped me to remember that both my parents were amateur painters themselves, and since I alone among their children had inherited the gene, I liked to think that drawing linked us in a primordial way.

At the beginning of high school, the Academy forced us to pick which subjects to pursue seriously and which to drop forever. Art was the first to go, my temple of safety violently demolished to make way for a monolith to biology built on my mother's vague hope that I might someday become an anesthesiologist. Now officially barred from attending any art classes during school hours, I channeled my silent frustration into drawing superheroes onto whatever nearby surface I could find. Thus enters Surma.

Surma is the Urdu word for eyeliner, a nickname I gave him because of the sixties-style kohl he had worn to school ever since first grade. The ancient tradition of children wearing black kohl on their inner eyelids has its roots in South Asia and North Africa as an antidote to the heat, but I always thought it made him looked like a hard-partying nineties supermodel. Surma was a painfully skinny child with long limbs and straight hair that lay flat across his unibrow like the ridge of a sharp cliff. He had been forced to sit next to me since grade two, a coincidence we resented for different reasons. Surma's family was ostentatiously religious; the father sported a long, white beard and had an amber rosary surgically grafted to his right hand, while the mother wore a black burqa so all-encompassing she looked like an angry shadow at parent-teacher meetings. Perhaps they are why Surma made it his personal crusade to invigilate the piety of people around him. The added benediction of the school's Islamiyat Department conferred upon Surma the halo of moral authority among the student body at large, and for some years it was as if God himself had anointed a boy-prophet at school with a penchant for a smoky eye. Don't know if you should brush your teeth during a fast? Ask Surma. Didn't know how many times you should pray today? Ask Surma. Unsure whether SuperCrisps are halal or not? Surma's your guy. For reasons tangentially related to religious traditions, Surma also came to school every morning with coconut oil in his hair, and I'd forever be wiping our shared desk with wet tissues to get rid of his oily fingermarks as he, in turn, did to my desk doodles. I still think of him whenever I catch a whiff of coconut tanning oil on a sandy beach, or, ironically, rum.

During the spring term of ninth grade, Surma and I sat sweating in the stiflingly hot classroom as the Islamic studies teacher droned on about the difference between archangels and the merely winged. Bored, I began drawing figures in my course book.

"Can you give them life?" Surma whispered, angrily tapping my drawings with his oily finger.

"Well," I said, considering my drawing of Angela Bassett reimagined as Storm. "In a way I already did. You know Michelangelo said—"

"These are *haram*!" he hissed. "Nothing but idolatry and a sin against our God!"

"I don't think I can breathe life into anything," I said. "I mean just yesterday there was a *Baywatch Hawaii* marathon on TV in which all they did was suck face, save lives, and run slowly. And honestly, Surma, all I was thinking the whole time was does CPR work if your breath stinks? Like, do you think lifeguards keep a pack of mints in their thongs just in case or is bad breath something one forgives in the euphoria of survival?"

"On the Day of Judgment," he muttered, holding both hands up to the sky in prayer. "God himself will throw you, along with your perverted drawings, into the deepest fires of the Devil's fury!"

"In that case," I said, adding a few strokes to Storm's bust, "she'll definitely need a sports bra . . ."

Surma changed desks that day. Like adult acne, he'll make an unwelcome appearance later in our story. But Surma wasn't the only one who found drawing offensive. There was a pervasive idea among my teachers and mother that art was a "girly subject" devoid somehow of the penile power of physics, the brute brawn of biology or the muscular machismo of mathematics. To admit that I wanted to study art at all felt tantamount to declaring I was gay, so I didn't. Jibran bypassed this particular hurdle by being superb at calculus.

We weren't as alone as we felt. Over the years I'd cataloged an archive of other girly boys at school—it didn't take much to spot us, a flimsy wrist here, a look of resigned terror there—but we pretended not to notice each other whenever we crossed paths in the noisy hallways since bitter experience had taught us that gathering in groups attracted violent attention. Still, it was hard not to notice Noor.

Noor's effeminacy was so bright that even from a distance he looked as out of place at the Academy as a ballerina on a rugby pitch. I'd sometimes catch sight of him gliding down the rowdy hallways in between classes like a bored runway model, taking slow deliberate steps in an absolutely straight line, arms motionless at his side, every inch of him singularly focused on how best to ignore the screaming students around him. He resembled the faces in his paintings: high cheekbones, feline eyes, aquiline nose. Seeing how deferentially the student body treated Noor because of his drawings—a mixture of respect, incredulity, and carnal desire—was the first time I realized that talent could be a weapon of self-defense too.

Notoriously shy, Noor spent most of his time with a recent transfer to the Academy, a boy named Ayaan who also happened to be one of my distant relatives in Lahore. We had always been friendly, Ayaan and I, but he had attended a different school, which at that age might as well be a different planet, and we rarely met outside of the yearly Eid lunches where he mimicked Daffy Duck. They made an unusual pair. Noor was quiet, delicate, and painfully reserved; Ayaan was tall, loud, and boisterously confident. Anyone who didn't know them would find it hard to imagine what the two had in common other that they both studied art.

I managed to make it a single, miserable year away from painting before I snapped and marched into the secluded art room to demand the teacher let me paint. The art room was housed in an old science lab, a dark cavernous hall still littered with dry sinks and broken beakers, its vast proportions far too grand for the paltry number of students who actually used it. In the center stood a sprawling wooden table around which dozens of desks had been pushed up against the walls to create space for metal easels and still-life arrangements, nearly every surface crusted with blotches of dried paint or stained with multicolored ink. It smelled like turpentine and freedom, and was the sole domain of Mr. Tasveer, a thin man with a mop of wiry hair who usually sat behind a large desk angled to guard the treasure of pristine art supplies he kept locked up in an oak armoire behind him.

As I entered the art room on that first day, I saw Ayaan and Noor drawing at the center table. Ayaan waved at me and bent over to whisper something in Noor's ear, who shot me an impassive glance before returning to his painting of three nude witches dancing around a fire pit. Mr. Tasveer was suspicious of my midterm desperation to join his class (it was a commonly held belief that art class was an easy A) and, wanting to be sure of my skill and genuine interest, gave me a sheet of paper and asked me to draw my favorite animal. I took a seat at the far end of the room and got to work in silence.

"That's very good," Noor said an hour later, leaning over my shoulder to consider my sketch. "Like, *really* good! Where did you learn to draw mermaids?" He motioned to Ayaan, who had been wrestling without success with the abstraction of a vase, to come and look.

"Oh, she's *always* had hidden talents," Ayaan said, putting on a camp American accent. "Haven't you, *dahling?*"

I knew that being called "she" was far from a slur, and I rolled my eyes playfully.

"I learned from books, mainly," I replied to Noor. "And *The Little Mermaid,* of course."

"Oh my God, I *love The Little Mermaid*! Have you seen the original one where she dies at the end and turns into foam? Ugh!" Noor pirouetted on the spot clutching a wine bottle full of linseed oil to his chest like a lost lover. "So romantic!"

"I know every word!"

"Bet you do, sea witch," Ayaan quipped.

"That's right, Christie," I replied in a mean voice, quoting a movie I'd just seen. "Keep telling yourself that . . ."

Both boys stared at me dumbstruck for a moment and then burst out laughing.

"Bitch!"

"Oh my god!"

"You've seen *Romy and Michele*?!"

"Who hasn't?" I said, burying my surprise that they recognized my most recent discovery.

"How have we not *met* before!" Noor said, sliding gracefully into the seat to my right.

"Told ya!" Ayaan said, crashing into a chair to my left. "Hidden talents!"

Mr. Tasveer confirmed my talent, and by the next week I was spending every moment I could in the art room. No one else was allowed inside except us, and over the years the room became a refuge of camp movie dialogues and gender-bending jokes. Jibran took my new friends in stride, and eventually he too joined the table for coffee, conversation, and compositional drawing.

We all loved *Romy and Michele's High School Reunion*, a movie so gloriously gay that it doesn't even have gay characters in it. From the pastel pantsuits of the mean girls to the interpretive dance set to Cindy Lauper's "Time After Time," it is, I still believe, a perfect film, not least because it allowed us to get through the terror of high school by pretending we already had. None of this horror was real, the film implied, it was only a passing phase on the road to glory and a ten-year contract with MGM (Turner Classic Movies gave me a vivid but dated view of how Hollywood worked). Recasting the threatening thugs around us as the midlevel bureaucrats they were destined to become was a strangely effective salve to their taunts.

My personal hero from the film was Heather Mooney. Seeing this foul-mouthed, chain-smoking goth harpy terrorize her way past her high school bullies felt like a sign that one day this punitive penitentiary would be a distant memory buried under the success of a publicly traded lifestyle company.

"Ignore them," Noor said to me in my junior year as a group of rowdy boys chanted "faggots" as us through the glass doors of the art room. "They're losers."

My assumption that he was immune from bullying had turned out to be a dark fiction. If my effeminacy invited ridicule, Noor's inspired a level of sexualized obsession that bordered on dangerous. To most students, Noor, effeminate and beautiful as he was, was the closest thing to a "girl" they could hope to encounter at school, and boys of all ages were unembarrassed to leave love letters at his desk or catcall obscenities as he strode by them. Even some of the teachers talked about him in class. He ignored these violations with grace and dignity, but whenever I saw them pick on him, I felt irate and fiercely protective of a kid who I knew had more talent in his little finger than the whole student body did combined.

"Scram, motherfuckers!" Ayaan's voice boomed from the other side of the corridor. "Or I'll send you to detention for so long your balls will shrivel up!" The bullies scurried away at his approach like frightened mice, and Ayaan continued to glare at them in his I'm-a-school-prefect-so-fear-me posture until they turned the corner, his jaw set and fists clenched tight. I was often envious that Ayaan's skill at mimicry also allowed him to perfectly impersonate the kind of macho murderous rage the Academy students considered real strength. It was easier to beat them in their own system, he explained to me years later, but there is always a price. Once he was sure our abusers had fled, Ayaan swung open the twin doors of the art room with a theatrical flourish.

"Come on, girls!" he sang, hips to one side, jazz hands splayed above. "Do you believe in love?"

"Cause I got something to say about it," Noor continued without glancing up.

"And it goes something like this!" I finished.

gay shrieks

Many of us develop defense mechanisms so deep and ruthless during the battles of high school that it takes years of therapy and the pain of many consequences to uproot them. Your teenaged years are a uniquely treacherous stretch of life, but if you're lucky, you do not tread them alone. And it is in that unlikely prison that I found the family—Jibran, Noor, and Ayaan—that would walk with me, hand in manicured hand, for decades to come.

Chapter 5

FOR GOD'S SAKE

*M*ANY PEOPLE HAVE WRITTEN ABOUT the cultural significance of *Buffy the Vampire Slayer*, the TV show that cleverly reframed the damsel in distress as the nightmare of monsters, but the weekly episodes I saw on TV in Pakistan were more to me than mere adolescent fang fantasy. Already feeling crushed under the unrelenting weight of oppressive religiosity in the Islamic Republic, shows like *Buffy* became a safe place to acknowledge my growing discontent with the fact that all the trappings of life—school, professions, marriage, but most of all religion—were meant for straight people, not folks like me. We were outcasts, fundamentally ineligible for God's benediction by the sin of our existence. The right to spirituality is often one of the first things stolen from queer people.

Like my own inner world of musical interludes and bitter monologues, the universe of *Buffy* also existed in the shadows of mainstream reality, a multidimensional, intersectional traffic jam deliberately hidden but altogether more important. One of the main characters in the show, Willow, evolves over the seasons from bookish nerd to godlike lesbian witch, and I cannot overemphasize what seeing a Wiccan lesbian relationship play out on primetime Pakistani cable TV every week did for my sense of possibility. But beyond simple representation, *Buffy* also allowed me the confidence to explore different religious faiths while living in a country built on the presumption that there can be only one.

Ours was never a staunchly religious family, but in Pakistan—founded as it was as a homeland for the Muslims of British-occupied India—everything is filtered through the prism of organized religion (Israelis know what I mean, don't you, girls?). My lifelong struggle with Islam's role in my own life was not simply that I felt excluded for being gay, but also that my home—a sanctuary where my mother read tarot cards every Wednesday, my father cooked Christmas puddings, and the family draped garlands of marigolds on the shoulders of Ganesh on Diwali—was so markedly different from the performative and often exclusionary religiosity I encountered outside. Sunni Islamic customs inform practically every aspect of life in Pakistan and, if the clerics are to be believed, most of the afterlife too. I grew up with a buffet approach to personal faith: picking up this, dropping that, getting really sick from those. But there was—is—no space to question the validity of following medieval moral philosophies in the Modern Age without also threatening to unravel everything that was supposedly keeping the country's tattered body politic together. That I cannot write that simple observation in most places in the world without the fear of violent retribution is part of the problem.

My gayness was never mutually exclusive to my personal faith (even as a child I knew that God, whoever she was, adored me) and I would later remind sanctimonious Americans of this fact during the War on Terror years just to see them turn purple. I've thought often and deeply about my relationship with divinity throughout my life and work, because to justify their hate, homophobes often rely on the idea that homosexuals have no innate claim to God. The insistence that we be excluded from traditional faith (so often a euphemism for "power") is a tool to ostracize us from mainstream institutions and, consequently, mainstream life. After all, it's easier to justify your irrational hate of a whole group of people if you believe that your hate is divinely mandated by a vengeful deity and not a product of your own twisted soul.

Buffy's world—a multiverse of multiple gods, witches, demons, magics, religions, and truths—felt not only familiar but aspirational. If I had been born a creature so fundamentally repulsive to the religion of my birth, was there perhaps another faith out there that did want me? The question eventually led me to research alternative religions in earnest, and I spent a fruitful two years toward the end of high school as a practicing Wiccan (shout-out to *The Craft*). I suppose Americans would call it a goth phase, but my interest in the occult extended beyond eye pencils and pentagram corsets (if only one could buy those in Lahore . . .).

In retrospect, openly acknowledging at age sixteen to anyone at a Pakistani high school that I was practicing a religion other than Islam was its own sort of coming out, though it helped that being raised as a Shia Muslim meant I already knew Islam had shades. Shia Muslims constitute a small but well-dressed minority in Pakistan, conspicuously set apart from the mainstream Sunni majority. The most obvious assertion of my being a Shia child (I'm sorry, I just can't bring myself to say Shi'ite) came every morning at daily school assembly. My grandmother had taught me that during any Quranic recitations I was supposed to keep my hands limp by my sides because that was what Shias did. I followed her instructions first out of deference, then out of defiance, and finally out of decision. This was not an easy thing to pull off surrounded by nine hundred boys, each with their hands overlapped dutifully at their navels in the Sunni style, the mass of them making me feel like a slutty Jezebel at the Islamic Ball.

Scanning the crowd, I'd spot an occasional break in the rows of folded hands, a confirmed sighting of Another from the UnFold. And for most of the year this remained the only discernible indicator of a child's religious identity, until the beginning of Muharram. It now seems symbolic to me that the most depressing month of Islam, a month in which stories of massacres, child murders, torture, and endless cruelty are told and retold, is also the first of its calendar.

Unhappy New Year, if you will.

The first ten days of Muharram, the Shia high holy days, are when they commemorate through ritualized storytelling the murders of the Prophet Muhammad's grandsons and his family at the hands of the then ruler, a Muslim named Yazid. My mother would take me with her to the narrow lanes of Lahore's medieval Old City for *majlis* to hear these stories. It was here that I experienced a communal religious identity that had nothing to do with my sexuality.

Well, almost nothing.

sips tea

Like most religious events in Pakistan, *majlis* is conspicuously segregated by gender, and while ordinarily I would chafe at being banished from the air-conditioned, perfumed comfort of the women's section to join the men's sauna of toe sweat outside, Muharram was altogether different. One of the rituals of mourning Shias observe is *maatam*, the symbolic beating of the chest to demonstrate grief. Women do this indoors away from prying eyes, but the men make a spectacle of their flagellation, standing in lines and beating their bare, sweaty pecs to the beat of drums. Some even use chains and knives to demonstrate their corporeal devotion.

Dhum, Dhum, Dhum.

The rhythm of the mourning song blared over the crackling loud-speakers. As a child, I meandered through a forest of legs to steal a view of the front row, where the strongest young men set the pace for the others. Men's calloused hands rose up in unison to the sky, sweaty back muscles glistening in the dusty sunlight, before swinging back down to hit their chests with a violent thud. On they'd go, one hand following the other, again and again until sweat turned to blood.

Dhum! Dhum! Dhum!

The pace would pick up as the *majlis* progressed until at its zenith a crowd of thousands stood beating their chests in fever-pitched synchronicity, the sound of their collective wailing rising up like a warsong. Years later, when I studied the queer undertones in the depiction of Saint Sebastian, or the work of artists like Tom of Finland and Robert Mapplethorpe, it was with a deep sense of corporeal familiarity.

Majlis was also the only place I ever saw grown men cry openly and without embarrassment. Those early experiences remain the most powerful expression of faith I've seen, in Pakistan or anywhere else. But it was the stories that I heard—the stories of Imam Hussain standing up for what was right rather than what was easy—that gave me a reservoir of strength in my own otherness. Because during Muharram I didn't feel othered. For once I didn't feel fat, or gay, or anglicized, or effeminate; all I felt was Shia, just another mourner in a great throng of visibly emotional people looking for a little catharsis. I felt, on reflection, included.

Once when I was about eight, as we made our way back from a *majlis* through the bloodied streets, I felt a pull on my *kameez* and turned to see a very old woman staring at me. She held up her tiny wrists, which were bound by handcuffs that were connected by chains to a pair of rusted manacles around her ankles. Her hair was a filthy, matted mess, her threadbare clothes stained and grubby, her bony feet blackened and bare.

"Please," she said. "Please undo them."

I was too scared to respond.

"It's OK," my mother whispered in my ear. "She won't hurt you."

"What does she want me to do?"

"She wants you to unlock her chains."

"But I don't have the keys."

Mother smiled. "They're not really locked, see?"

"Why can't she open them herself?"

"She believes only a Syed can undo them for her," Ma said. "A descendant of the prophet," she added when I didn't understand.

The woman stood as we spoke, arms still outstretched. "Please?" she asked me again.

Even at eight, I remember thinking the claim that there was a genealogical line from the Prophet to me laughable. It sounded like all the other tall tales of storied ancestry people in South Asia often spun for invented self-importance. But I stepped forward and held her brittle wrists in my hand to unclasp them. The metal rings fell to the ground with a dull clang and she exhaled a long, guttural sigh of relief.

"Thank you," she said, tears streaming down the canyons of her crow's feet. "May God grant you happiness." I would undo her chains every year for the next several years until one Muharram, I couldn't find her. "God probably granted her wish," my mother said when I asked her about it. "That's why she'd been wearing the chains in the first place. They were a symbol of her prayer to God. It's like a spell, if you think about it."

South Asia is full of magic. It is in the way people avoid walking under trees at night so as not to wake up sleeping spirits. It's in the Arabic phrase "mashallah" scrawled onto to the pediments of Corinthian houses all over Pakistan as an enchantment meant to ward off envy. It's in the written incantations wise men cram into leather talismans to cure everything from impotence to broken phones. It's in my grandfather's turquoise ring that he wore to ward off the evil eye, and in my mother's insistence to always give some money to charity every time she travels as *sadka*. When I think of my faith (as European Americans so often demand Muslims living in America do), I think of these things, as much a part of the fabric of my soul as my first kiss.

Most Pakistanis could tell I was Shia from my name alone, which painted yet another round target on my expansive backside. The ninth and tenth days of Muharram (the holiest of the ten days) are a national holiday in Pakistan, a relic from a tolerant past long since under siege, and I dreaded going back to school the next day because there was always a paranoid hemorrhoid waiting to heckle me.

"*Kaafir!*"

"Infidel!"

"Did your mom cut herself too!"

"You're going to go to hell!"

I don't think they realized what a relief it was to be bullied for something as simple as sectarian difference. One day in freshman year a boy got carried away and, to impress the silent crowd, moved to hit me for being a "nonbeliever." I closed my eyes and waited. When nothing happened, I opened them to see him face down in the mud being beaten by a burly senior several years older than us both.

"Never!" the older boy shouted, punctuating each word with an open-palm slap across the bully's face. "Touch! One! Of! Us! Again! Understand?!"

Five of his even larger friends stood behind him, ready for battle should anyone intervene on my bully's behalf. No one dared.

My muscular rescuer approached me afterward.

"You OK?" he asked me, wiping the mud off his hand. I recognized his face from the crowds at *majlis*, but we'd never actually met. He pushed away a lock of dark hair from his eyes, and I saw he wore the same silver bracelet on his right wrist as I did.

"Are you OK?" he repeated.

"Y-yes," I said, stunned that he cared.

"If he ever bothers you again, you let me know, huh?" he said, and flashed me a bright smile. "*Ya Ali madad!*"

"The Shia mafia," Jibran said as we watched them walk away, "is an *extremely* useful group to know."

But by junior year I had stopped waiting for anyone to save me, muscular or otherwise. The path to my salvation seemed clear: use whatever means I could to achieve as much as possible in this rotten, rotting system so I could one day escape and never return. Since my accent in English made me sound like a tart duchess (thank you, *My Fair Lady*), teachers began choosing me to represent the Academy at debating competitions all over Lahore. Overnight I found my devotion to memorizing bitchy asides and gay witticisms finally began to pay off in awards, medals, and trophies. The light of these public successes made me conspicuous, if not popular, and kept most bullying away. For the rest, I weaponized my tongue into an instrument of cruelty, as capable of getting a laugh as drawing blood. Now if some hulking cricketer tried to make fun of me in class for my weight or effeminacy, it was easy to twist his words into a noose around his dimwitted neck until he became the butt of the joke himself. Often I went too far, striking out with an arsenal of ugly classism, elitist disdain, and public humiliation, using absolutely anything I could think of to make my opponent feel as terrible about themselves as I did. I was too consumed with my own victimhood at the time to reflect on how my own privilege—family name, social access, the presumption that I would be sent abroad for college—affected how I navigated school or was thought of by the other students. Whatever social advantage I had felt like a mirage compared to the concrete ridicule I faced for being gay.

But new things began to matter once we were upperclassmen, like how many girls you were friends with outside the Academy, or how many coed parties you could get invited to at the houses of kids whose parents drank alcohol. The bullies and sportsmen who had dominated life at school so far suddenly found themselves at a severe social disadvantage for, unlike me, they did not meet girls from other schools at their competitions, and kicking a football in a country without cheerleaders did little to expand their social opportunities.

Whatever I lacked in athletic ability I now made up for in extra-curricular enthusiasm, and there was scarcely a school club or English-speaking competition I didn't aim to dominate: essay writing, poetry recitals, painting competitions, yearbook editing, photography club, spelling bees, parliamentary debates—if it meant skipping math class, I was there like green on grass.

By now my family had moved from our small town house and into a larger home in a new development far away from Zariyan's. We hadn't spoken since the incident at the parking lot, a fact made easier by his expulsion from school shortly after for failing his exams, a fact I only discovered because the school posted everyone's grades on the notice board to publicly traumatize academic underachievers. I heard that he eventually rode his American passport to a new life, and I buried my memories of us deep beneath an ocean of shame. *I'm not really gay*, I told myself whenever I saw the bathers in the Canal now. *That's just the only body I've been allowed to explore. When I get a girlfriend, everything will be fine.* And I believed it too, not because I thought it was true, but because my soul felt so much lighter without the self-loathing.

At the tail end of junior year, Jibran and I were sitting on a bench outside class during a free period when a friendly English teacher walked by.

"Who died?" Jibran asked, noticing her unusually morbid ensemble.

"*Ufff!*" she said, raising a manicured hand to her cheek. "So sad! So young! Such a *tragedy!*"

"What happened?" we asked.

"Do you remember a boy called Zariyan? Short, skinny, here a few years ago? No? Anyway, last night the father walked into the room and found the body. Apparently he—"

They kept talking, both too busy trying to place him to notice my world had ended.

"Um," I asked, the drum of my heartbeat thumping in my ear. "What's his name again?"

"Her," the teacher clarified. Zariyan's sister had died in the middle of the night of an aneurism. She was twenty.

"Are you all right?" Jibran asked when he saw my face. "You don't look so good."

"M'fine," I muttered, "I just have to . . ." and walked in a daze to the lesser used bathrooms behind the biology labs. The usual student smokers weren't there yet, so I bolted the wooden door shut and stood at the row of stained sinks staring at my reflection in a dirty mirror. My breathing became shallower until it felt like there was no air left inside my lungs at all and I fell on the filthy floor, dry heaving as the locked memories of my childhood battered me with the force of a galloping flood. There was no corner left in my mind to hide in anymore. I knew that I had loved him, which came as somewhat of a surprise to me because "love" was not a word I used often. That love so often condemned to the purgatory of silence was confusing, toxic, and hurtful, yes, but it was also vivid, unvarnished, and real. I knew how much he'd loved his sister, how much he'd loved only her, just as I knew that I could never bring myself to see him again. I stayed in the locked bathroom until the panic attack subsided and the nicotine addicts began banging at the door. When I reached home that day my parents were already on their way to the funeral.

"Aren't you coming with us?" my father asked me.

"No," I said.

"It'll be very rude of you," my mother added. "Didn't you play with her brother as a child?"

"I did," I said, and walked inside the house.

Chapter 6

MONSOON WEDDING

*J*UST BEFORE THE START OF our senior year, Jibran told me he wouldn't be returning to the Academy; his family was immigrating to Canada, and he'd finish high school there. I had already said my goodbyes to Noor and Ayaan before they left to begin college in America (they were a year ahead), but losing Jibran had been a painful surprise.

"I'll still call you all the time," he promised. A solid silence rose to fill the space between us not already occupied by the Dungeons & Dragons campaign we'd been waging.

"I don't know what I'm going to do without you," I said. Losing him felt like an amputation of the only part of me that had felt true.

"I know," he whispered. "Me too."

I was too preoccupied with selfish thoughts to notice that Jibran wore the same terrified expression he had before any Urdu exam. It was some time before he shook the doubt from his head.

"I have to tell you something and it'sreallyreallyimportant." His words flew past me in an anxious arrow. Jibran's eyes remained fixed on the gold satin bedspread below us, the same one we had bought together from the flea market after seeing *Cleopatra* for the first time ("I see you baby, shaking that asp").

"Oh, God," I moaned. "What now? You won a million dollars? Streisand is your music coach? They're doing *Cabaret* at your new high school? For the love of Oprah, WHAT?"

"I'm—I'm gay," he said, and his hand shot up to his mouth as if it had spoken without permission. I followed his large eyes darting around the room until they slowly found mine. We stared at each other for a beat, both of us shocked by the audacity of confirming a commonality that had been ever-implied but never declared.

It was time to, in the words of the classic Celine Dion–Barbra Streisand duet, tell him.

"Join the club!"

A heady euphoria washed over us as we collapsed into a messy, teary hug. Only other queer people know the power of this moment, that indescribable rush of joy, belonging, excitement, and relief we feel when we are finally able to say out loud what we've been forced to hide inside for so very long. It feels like diving off a cliff you've been dreading only to discover you can fly. A light flicks on in the darkness, the monsters scurry away, and for one brief, peaceful moment, you are free.

Shortly afterward I came out to both Noor and Ayaan on the phone ("So . . . who are you sleeping with?"), and it's a testament to the innate authenticity of my friendships that coming out to each other changed very little in our regular conversation. Sure, we could now openly talk about the cricket captain's perfect ass, but none of us had really pretended to be straight with each other in the first place. Finally free of the last fears that bound us in silence, Jibran and I spent the night gossiping about important things like school crushes, imaginary boyfriends, and which bride looked the tackiest at the latest string of Lahori weddings.

"I knew it!" Jibran said when I confirmed my sophomore-year crush. Being in the closet hadn't stopped me from embarking on the most devastating one-sided relationships with a slew of unavailable straight boys at school who had no idea I existed, which is, I believe, a rite of gay passage. Indeed, I had so many crushes that after a while it was easier to nickname each of them "the Diamond," my homage to Nicole Kidman's character in *Moulin Rouge*.

"Without the corsetry," Jibran noted. "But full marks for the reference." I finally opened up to him about my sexual history with Zariyan and waited, as all teenage friends do, for the confirmation that I had won our silent game of comparison.

"All that time and I didn't even *know*!" He clapped his hands together in glee. "OK, OK, my turn! So, you know Bilal from class?"

"Billionaire Bilal, Bully Bilal, or Bucktoothed Bilal?"

"Bully Bilal," he said.

"Yes . . ." I said suspiciously. "What about him?"

Of the various acquaintances Jibran and I had maintained over the years, Bilal Sadiq was by far the worst. We'd briefly bonded in middle school over a shared love of Alanis Morissette, but then we entered high school and Bilal fell in with a group of varsity athletes, after which he used us as target practice for his burgeoning homophobia.

"We've been sleeping together for four years!" Jibran screeched.

It's a rare thing to actually feel fate's handprint lingering on your cheek after a good bitch slap.

"B-but," I stuttered, trying to piece together a timeline where this made any sense. "But he's so mean to you!" I reminded him that barely weeks before I had walked into our school play rehearsals to find Bilal leading a chant of "Faggot! Faggot!" as Jibran tried to finish his monologue as Mrs. White from *Clue*, but Jibran simply shrugged.

"He's nice behind closed doors," he said. We moved on to other topics, like if he ever thought about telling his parents one day, or how wonderful it was going to be in Canada. I played along, but Bully Bilal's behavior had lit an inferno of indignation inside me. It wasn't simply that he was a bully; bullies I could handle. No, this bitch was a traitor. And if reading *The Chronicles of Narnia* had taught me any lesson as a child besides the importance of packing thermal underwear, it was that traitors must pay.

Senior year found me as alone at home as at school. Both my sisters now lived abroad, so it was only me with my parents in the house. I locked myself in my bedroom to better focus on the raging anxiety of SAT prep and US college applications in solitude. It helped that my eldest sister was going to be married in spring, and my parents were preoccupied with planning the event. I worked on my applications as best I could and sent them off with hopeful excitement. On the windy spring night of the actual wedding several months later, I fell spectacularly ill with a stomach flu. South Asian stomach bugs are not mild conditions, the kind of serene illnesses that allow you to recline gracefully on a Victorian fainting couch while kindly matrons press bottles of smelling salts up to your nose. No, these are intestinal demons that turn your toilet into Chernobyl.

I returned from the hospital a mere hour before that night's *mehndi* was due to start, still retching but somewhat rested after a restorative IV drip. My father was outside arguing with the florists while my mother was sitting on the living room couch chanting into a mound of dough, performing a spell her grandmother gave her to keep rain away on important occasions, which, judging by the dark clouds swirling outside, wasn't working spectacularly well. The house felt tense, as it usually did around special occasions. This was the first wedding in our immediate family. Everyone was nervous.

By 2002 Pakistan had moved on from Pulse Global tapes. Three years earlier, yet another overweight military dictator named Musharraf had couped his way to the crown (a chronic illness) and

then used unending televised speeches to convince the na
this had not been a Shitty Thing for him to do. Because of
reservoirs of money and temporary importance Bush's War on Terror
would shortly confer on Pakistan and its power-hungry army, the
country, for the most part, agreed.

Many changes quickly followed: The single state-run channel
Pakistan TV was now joined by hundreds of new channels that
blossomed under more lenient media laws. Newspapers flourished,
TV serials bloomed, and flamboyant fashion designers sent skinny
models down lopsided runways, convinced without evidence that
every stiletto stomp was a slap against the rising tide of extremism
pouring in from Afghanistan and Saudi Arabia.

At home, a gold-trimmed wedding tent was erected in the empty
plot next to our house and, after throwing up a few times in the
flower beds, I joined my family in the receiving line to greet the
hundreds of guests streaming inside wearing their best diamonds
and brightest silks.

I cannot stress enough to you how central weddings are to Pakistani culture. They are the Diana to our Supremes, the Dorothy to
our *Golden Girls*, they put the Fun in Fundamentalism. Ever since
Pakistan banned booze in the seventies as a short-sighted concession
to the religious right (that one would subsequently have to deal
with them entirely sober apparently never occurred to anyone),
weddings are essentially all we do. Given that non-Muslims are
technically allowed to buy alcohol in the country, there are actually
some good distilleries in Pakistan. My favorite local spirit is called
Murree's Sapphire gin. From a distance, it designed to look like a
bottle of Bombay Sapphire, but a closer inspection confirms that
this Ms. Sapphire fell on hard times, pawned her larger jewels for
rent, and now works at a plastic recycling plant sorting discarded
take-out containers. I love it anyway because with Murree gin it's

not the glass bottle but the alcohol itself that is dyed a bright, incandescent blue.

If you drink enough your pee turns turquoise the next day.

When people discover that Pakistan doesn't serve alcohol legally, they either imagine a romanticized Prohibition-era cocktail orgy or else a dry tundra of judgmental teetotalers. The truth is less romantic than either. The generation that grew up before the ban speaks nostalgically of glittering masquerade balls held at private clubs and champagne flute dinners at hotel bars, nearly always airily glossing over their generation's active role in the loss of all those things. The rest of us in the prohibitive present are forced to rely on jumpy, overpriced bootleggers. Most of them come in their own transport, nondescript vehicles cleverly retrofitted with smugglers holes so that police checkpoints won't spot the whiskey bottle hidden behind the rearview mirror. Others are more inventive, like the elderly man who could produce bottles of chilled Grey Goose from within his wooden leg. At times like that, when you're paying wildly inflated prices for a bottle of vodka that traveled to you in an appendage, needing a drink in the Islamic Republic can feel like being the only incurable resident at the Betty Ford clinic.

Pakistan has little public life that doesn't involve clapping for the armed forces or God, so a well-planned wedding fulfills the function of a matchmaking event, disco, restaurant opening, corporate retreat, nightclub, school prom, dance recital, fashion show, charity fete, and, in the case of the better ones, an open bar.

Unlike some of the marriages, desi weddings are not short affairs. It's quite normal for a single couple to invite you to up to eight ceremonies—more if you've actually met either of them—and the numbers add up quickly. Say you're in your midtwenties (#itgetsbetter) and you know six couples getting married one year. That's already forty-eight individual events, all overlapping with one another in the span of four manic, overdressed December weekends (only the very rich or the very mad get married in the summer heat, often to each other). By the end of the wedding season, it feels like you've been gangbanged by sequins.

Given the centrality of getting hitched, it's not that surprising that the first movie to show an upper-middle-class South Asian family on-screen with any measure of realism also revolved around a, you guessed it, wedding. Most Bollywood movies descend into the nauseating pit of nuptials, of course, but something about sari-clad brides forced to lip-synch on Swiss glaciers makes one doubt realism is a guiding principle. *Monsoon Wedding* was different—a realistic, tense, joyous explosion of a film that was set in a world so deeply familiar to me that watching it left me feeling less seen than caught. The bride's younger brother in the movie, to pluck a triggering petal from the marigolds, was also a pudgy, effeminate English-speaking brown kid whose love of dance and cooking made his doting parents question his sexuality.

"He's just like you," mothers across South Asia commented to their closeted sons.

"Mmmm," we all mumbled back.

No one ever talked about that character being gay per se. No one ever talked about being gay at all, really, even though I saw more homosexual desire around me than not. It was perfectly normal, for instance, to see two boys at school or two men on the street in Lahore walking together with their hands intertwined like lovers. For an unmarried heterosexual couple to do the same was, by comparison, nearly unthinkable. College professors later called places like Morocco, Pakistan, and India "homosocial environments," societies where the cultural separation of genders meant public affection between men became an act of social conformity to segregation rather than any conscious declaration of an individual sexual identity. In places like these, the segregation confers a sense of plausible deniability on homosexual relationships. After all, hiding in plain sight is one of the ways that queer people can live with some measure of agency in repressive states the world over (how else do you think we got through the Middle Ages?). How can you be gay where gayness doesn't exist?

This lazy conceit works right up until boys are expected to marry, which is usually when things fall spectacularly to pieces. Most of the gay men I know in Pakistan, even Western-educated, quasi-liberal ones living in the twenty-first century—unclench, I'm not outing you—are intent on marrying women. These men rarely call themselves gay (though enough of their ex-wives do) because to do that would require an acknowledgment of a reality they've worked extraordinarily hard to deny. It's sad but not incomprehensible that in a feudal country where most people are raised in clannish joint-family systems (a euphemism for when codependency becomes a parenting strategy), a homosexual man would choose to conform to the social contract rather than confront it and risk expulsion. Some do it to maintain their hold on family properties, others do it because of intense self-loathing, but most do it because they know no other way to live.

There are some exceptions, mostly gay men from the upper classes who wrap themselves in the embroidered privilege of their position to live their lives with some measure of authenticity. They are tolerated because they are not seen as a threat so much as neutered courtiers in this cruel kingdom. I used to think of closeted men in South Asia like the White Witch from Narnia: angry, frigid queens trapped inside vast closets where it was always winter but never Christmas. We've never gotten along. They think I'm dangerous and naive, I think they're cowards and hypocrites, resentful only that they can't take on a more powerful role in the patriarchal system that oppresses us both. Homophobia is, I assure you, not exclusive to straight people.

"Soon it'll be your wedding, huh?" the aunties said as they squeezed my cheeks between their jeweled pincers. "Have to find you a nice girl very soon!"

"Likewise!"

My favorite part of a wedding is called the *baraat*. It happens just before the main reception, when the groom's side arrives en masse with drummers and dancers, and the bride's side lines up to welcome them with a shower of flowers. The whole joyful mess then makes its way to a waiting stage where the couple sits together looking radiantly uncomfortable as everyone watches on misty-eyed. (Someone later holds the groom's shoe hostage for a large cash payment, but let's stay focused.)

As I absentmindedly flung rose petals at the strangers dancing past me—forefingers pointing up, jumping in circles on one foot to the beat by a frenzied drummer—I spotted my eldest sister laughing in the distance. She whispered something in my new brother-in-law's ear, and he grinned, and stole a quick kiss on her cheek before the next set of family friends came to pose for a photograph. Watching them, I felt an ache in my stomach that had nothing to do with the bug still churning inside me.

Will I ever have a wedding?

It was a dark premonition: me arriving sidesaddle on a tranquilized horse, Jibran, Noor, and Ayaan behind me, not walking so much as clumsily skipping to avoid getting horse shit on their shoes as my parents looked on in crumbling shame that I was not more popular. I could imagine no large clan of well-wishers, no sprawling tribe of cousins and no well-meaning coworkers to bolster my numbers. It wasn't simply guilt at not having enough bodies to fill the tent; it was the inkling that the rite of passage central to my culture—to all cultures, if we're honest—was also the embodiment of everything I was explicitly forbidden to want for myself. There would be no white horse for my wedding, no doting aunts or dramatic entrances; a thousand guests would not stream into a gold-trimmed tent to witness me profess my love in public as photographers clicked over-lit mementos destined for dusty velvet albums; there would be no chorus of off-key singers, no dinners for visiting foreign friends, no elaborately choreographed dances, no teary farewells. In the thick of these anxiety spirals I would occasionally try to scry the face of my future spouse, but even in my own wedding fantasies I was single.

The morning I saw Jibran off at the airport was also the first day of senior year, which was exactly like my first day at the Academy—terrifyingly lonely, emotionally abusive, and someone left a poo on the second-floor landing. But the energy of change in Jibran's life inspired me to build some momentum of my own, so I joined a new gym on a whim, the latest in a series of them that had opened to cater to Pakistan's newfound interest in weight training. I worked with a muscular trainer every day, and by my sister's wedding many months later, I had lost close to one hundred pounds of mostly cheesecake. My every rep was fueled by the prospect of an impending gay life at college abroad, and I was determined to be thin enough to fit into it.

Losing that much weight confirmed two things I'd long suspected but could never prove. One: there is no shortcut to losing weight. No, not even surgery. Yes, even that one. You have to burn more than you eat. It sucks, but there you have it. Two: thin people get treated better in this world at every turn. Like, you won't *believe* how much better. It helped that my weight loss coincided with an unexpected increase in my height that took me from hobbit to giant, and although my manboobs endured like two ancient pyramids weathering time and the Saharan winds, the rest of me finally began to approximate the body of a man, a change I was the last to notice. You'd think the pictures from the wedding would serve as a record of my triumph, but in most of them I look like Shrek after gastric bypass surgery. But compliments are very addictive, and as I went around the room snapping them up like coins in a video game, I spotted Bully Bilal standing between his doting parents. He caught me looking and sauntered over with a menacing sneer.

"Don't see any of *your* friends here," he said. As he made a show of craning his neck around the crowded tent, I considered him: groomed, perfumed, and wearing a monochromatic outfit he bragged about designing himself—I kicked myself for not having figured out his secret sooner.

"They're all abroad," I said, in a tone that I hoped implied I'd just landed from the Amalfi Coast myself.

"Or," Bully Bilal whispered, waving at a pretty girl in the distance, "maybe it's just that no one likes you." He looked me straight in the eye. "You fat fucking faggot." At that moment one of my sister's more glamorous friends shouted my name for our upcoming dance number.

"Pardon me," I whispered, channeling Sheila. "I have a show to do."

On the last day of high school, I sent Bully Bilal an email, subject line: "I know who you did last summer," and sat back in satisfied smugness as he immediately fired back emails, first threatening, then pleading with me to keep quiet. In the words of Madeline Ashton from the classic *Death Becomes Her*: "*These* are the moments that make life worth living!" He had no power over me now, of course; none of them did.

I tell you the story of Bully Bilal not to shame him so much as myself, because it is often your own who can hurt you the most.

In the years since being gay has gone from secret to sensation, the ethics of outing someone else has remained a touchy subject, even if they are gay homophobes who bullied you for years. As an obviously effeminate gay boy I couldn't hide my secret from other people. Consequently, others would either abuse me for it or, occasionally, confide in me about the flickers of rainbow in their own sexuality. At first, I thought this was because I was some homing beacon of homosexuality, but it was really because they thought me so inconsequential in the pecking order that to tell me something was the equivalent of telling no one. It's happened many times since then too, particularly with Pakistani men who assume I would stand as keeper to the covenant of their self-hatred. Very quickly the question for me in this context became not whether it's right or not for me to out someone who had weaponized homophobia for camouflage, but why the burden of someone else's secret should have been mine to bear at all, particularly when my own weight gave me sciatica.

The storm clouds above us burst and rainwater weighed down large parts of the wedding tent while violent gusts of winds forced other sections to billow up like the giant sails of a ship caught in a terrible storm. As the wind howled and the fairy lights flickered, anxious guests began to clump around the exits. I barely made it through two minutes of my dance routine before my stomach bug protested and I had to run off stage to throw up onto what I thought was a vase but turned out to be a five-year-old.

The tent's massive wooden center pole rose several feet from the ground with each new surge of wind. Within minutes the rain went from a torrent to a deluge. There was a loud groan as the main tent pole wobbled and then finally collapsed under the weight of pooling water, leaving five hundred overdressed Lahoris flailing in the downpour in front of a line of po-faced chauffeurs. I spotted my eldest sister weeping as her friends tried to comfort her. Someone rallied the drummers to start a beat outside, and people began dancing in the rain, deliriously happy and soaking wet.

"Just like *Monsoon Wedding*, innit!" said one of the visiting Englishmen as he spasmed past me.

"You have no idea," I moaned, and crawled off to find another flower arrangement to soil.

Chapter 7

SHE DOESN'T EVEN GO HERE!

AROUND DECEMBER 2001, ONCE THE shock of 9/11 had given way to America's thirst for revenge, our school guidance counselor warned rising seniors that US universities would likely sharply cut down on our acceptances. Things were going to get particularly difficult for male students from Muslim countries, he added, and he was right. In the next few admission cycles, only a handful of Academy students were accepted into foreign colleges, mainly those who already had US passports or enough money not to need one. Others found that even with a hard-won acceptance letter, their student visas languished unprocessed at the US embassy for months and months until it was too late to enroll anyway. Most didn't even bother applying.

While the institutionalized vilification of Muslims post 9/11 was a real concern for me before applying to colleges in North America, what actually terrified me the most was communal bathrooms. Teen movies and college brochures had long implied that students were expected to shower together in large chambers of ridicule—prison-style—rather than in individual cubicles of pristine modesty. The prospect of being naked in front of a room full of Abercrombie & Fitch lookalikes was so stressful that I imagined I'd rather just end it all and slit my wrists, arranging myself artfully on a gleaming, white-tiled floor, fully clothed in posthumous protest.

I'd thought about suicide a lot the summer before college. I wasn't accepted by the college I had planned to attend since I was ten (an obsession my therapist traces back to an unhealthy attachment to a Barbra Streisand movie) and the disappointment destroyed me. I'd internalized early on that any life that allowed me to be my true gay self could materialize only after studying at an Ivy League American college near New York City, and managing that feat had been my single-minded goal for as long as I could remember. But on April 1, 2003, the rejections poured into my Hotmail account like a herd of homicidal Hogwarts letters, each another painful cut into my rapidly hemorrhaging future.

Afterward I fell asleep within seconds, the kind of deep, bottomless slumber that comes when all strength is gone and the battle has been lost. It didn't make sense. I'd done everything I was meant to do: I'd suffered through the Academy, studied for my A's, got near-perfect SAT scores, and cut out carbs after six P.M. But for what? For as long as I could remember, the hope that I too could live out the glamorous lives I idolized in American movies had kept the worst of the darkness at bay. Born with a Pakistani passport, college was my one shot to make a life for myself in a place without oppressive religiosity and feudal posturing; a place where I could kiss a date on the street without the fear I'd be beaten or killed; a place where being gay wasn't a death sentence or, worse, a gray life lived in muted shadows; a place where I was not wrong for simply existing. I had believed for as long as I could believe anything that in order to be myself I had to leave Pakistan, but the letters had stolen that hope with the brevity of a word.

Rejected.

I woke up the next morning to the brief balm of nothingness before the memory of the rejections crashed over me. I lay back down under a thick blanket of pain, convinced that life itself was now forever over.

I would never be happy, I would never be free, I would never be me. My parents were crushed on my behalf. My father hugged me every time I passed him, and my mother did daily tarot readings, holding up any positive cards as proof that things would work out. Hope felt too painful, so I catastrophized what the next four years of my life would look like: I'd remain in Lahore for college, suffocating in the same thick fog of toxic masculinity that had been my school experience; I'd live at home and not a dorm; there would be no LGBT student mixers or freshman social games; eventually I'd be forced to choose an insipid degree like developmental economics because so few places offered anything else. And as for my love life? I'd probably have to smuggle dates masquerading as friends through the TV lounge as my parents watched us go into my room still plastered with *Buffy* posters and X-Men memorabilia. Assuming I met any boys at all.

I chose a night I knew the family would be out for dinner. Once I was sure I was alone, I nicked a butcher's knife from the kitchen and a bottle of pills from my mother's medicine cabinet and debated how exactly to kill myself. Pills were the obvious route, but what if I didn't take enough and just woke up with a really bad headache? OK. Knife, then. Ugh, though, all that blood. It would be so selfish to leave behind a mess, and my parents would have so much to explain anyway. OK. Pills, then. But how many?

Deeper and deeper I ricocheted down the welcoming circles of hell toward the temptation of an endless sleep. At some point, between my heaves and sobs, I caught background snippets of the movie *The Hours*, that ode to depression starring Meryl Streep, Julianne Moore, and Nicole Kidman's prosthetic nose.

"Just let me die," I said aloud to the emptiness, utterly exhausted by the relentless push of my negative thoughts. And as I gripped the bottle of pills one final time, resolved to silence the voices once and for all, I heard a faint whisper, soft as a feather but stiff as a board: *Hold on*, it said. *Just a little while longer. Hold on.*

Suicidal thoughts are powerful hallucinogens. They convince you that your future is not only bleak but nonexistent. The quicker you end yourself, the thoughts say, the quicker your pain will end too. I didn't have anyone around me at the time in whom I could confide why exactly I was so abysmally sad over college rejections because, like with everything else remotely authentic in my life, it would have meant confessing I was gay. For people witnessing a serious struggle in another, listing out logical reasons for why they shouldn't feel awful doesn't help. No one can say or do anything to make grief evaporate, but it does help for someone to acknowledge the fact of your pain. To sit in the current of sadness with you, without judgment, without words, without expectation, and tell you that it's OK to feel terrible when terrible things happen. From personal experience, it really helps if one of those people is Meryl Streep.

And so I held on, and awoke the next morning, battered but breathing, the unused knife in my hand, the closed pill box by my bedside. Outside, I could hear the muffled sounds of the household beginning another day—the dogs barking, my mother watching morning TV shows, my father chatting on the phone—and sighed in relief at just how unaware they were that my world had sewn itself back together with gossamer threads.

That night is the closest I've come to suicide. Contemplating whether to end our lives is depressingly common for many queer teens the world over. While our actions may have been triggered by different things—rejection letters, broken hearts, battered bodies— our struggles are no reason to feel shame. It is not our fault that we faltered under the unrelenting pressure of a world that preaches every day that we are not worthy of love. Discard shame; it's useless. Get angry instead. Irate that they made you think you were unworthy of love to begin with; enraged that someone as unique and special as you was told every single day—by parents, teachers, friends, cultures, countries, and gods—that your kind don't deserve happiness in this life unless you are exceptional in some way that is acceptable to them. Some people need you to believe that if you don't mutilate yourself for the sake of others, you're nothing but selfish and damned. Their hate is not your burden.

They—and I cannot stress this enough—can fuck all the way off.

Once anger has abated, it may be that you'll hobble on the cobbled path to solace. And beyond that, perhaps even to acceptance. Keep chasing the next best feeling and eventually, inevitably, you will arrive at peace. You will not stay here long. Something will drag you back into the pain of the world, but I promise you it gets easier to find your way back out again and again until one day, when you least suspect it, the peace becomes a part of you.

I returned to my last few months at the Academy hurt and humiliated, weathering the withering stares of boys brandishing their college acceptance letters like golden tickets to Willy Wonka's factory. I didn't react to the ridicule from classmates of my having failed to get into college or the pity from teachers. There was nothing left in me for them to beak.

The only thing I knew to do in the weeks that followed was to grip the memory of my near-suicide as close to me as possible. It became my talisman, symbolic not of what nearly defeated me but of what I survived. And then, one innocuous day in early May, I received a slim letter from a well-ranked college in Montreal whose silence I had mistaken for rejection.

"Congratulations, Komail! We are delighted to offer you a place in the class . . ."

I touched the words on the heavy cream paper to make sure they were real, that this wasn't some cruel trick or hallucination. But there, in embossed black lettering, was my ticket.

Jibran screamed in joy when I told him I'd be moving to Montreal, where he was already living. "We're are going to have so much fun!" His excitement reignited my own, and slowly my depression curled up in a dark corner inside me, dormant but watchful as I put the pieces of myself back together.

It was stunning how quickly life would begin to improve once I exited the daily oppression of the Academy, but before that happened, I was accused of blasphemy.

Twice.

The first time was because of Surma, our kohl-eyed vixen. Not content with policing my doodles, Surma had kept a hateful eye on me for years after our seating divorce and was very angry when I was appointed editor in chief of the school's thirteen publications instead of him (I later rigged the yearbook awards, so I won Most Talented and he won Least Likely to Get Laid). He got his revenge mere weeks before graduation by inciting the Islamic studies teachers to demand my immediate expulsion because I'd signed off on the printing of an anonymous poem in the English magazine titled "Princess Allah." I assume the objection was to Allah having a female gender and royal titles, but no one was forthcoming with specifics. As the headmaster shouted at me for my willful ignorance despite the "dangerous elements" overrunning the country around us, I spotted Surma lurking outside the office like a gecko and just *knew* who was responsible for the anonymous accusation. I agreed to withdraw the poem without debate because I had better parties to attend, and while this charge was dismissed quickly enough, the next one wasn't.

Once my parents realized that it was easier to let me take art as a subject than it was to pay the fines the school charged for all the physics classes I was skipping, I was allowed to keep studying art, but only after school. After I stood first in the country in my exams, I looked at both my parents as if to say, "Stop me now, I dare you."

As part of the senior year coursework, we (I use "we" here like a European megalomaniac, as I was the only person in art class) had to send a portfolio of drawings to be judged by examiners in England. My thesis was called "Fatty Feast: Gluttony at the South Asian Wedding," and with it I sent along a file thick with drawings of dinner scenes, serving platters, and, because I thought no one I knew would ever see it, several voluptuous self-portraits of my body. Most of the last third was just close-up drawings of my boob folds, if I'm honest. Midway through the summer after high school graduation, I was summoned back to the Academy with a cryptic text from my former headmaster. He told me that the government had impounded my drawings at customs on the way back into Pakistan on the grounds of indecency.

"That's from the federal government," he said, flinging a brown paper envelope across the desk. It was addressed to me and bore a holographic seal of a crescent next to a star. "Take it seriously."

The letter instructed me to appear before a tribunal at the Lahore airport a few weeks later. I downplayed the danger of the notice because there is only so much trauma one can face in the summer heat, but on the morning of the tribunal I shook with anxiety as I donned my school uniform for one last, loathsome time in the hope it would lend me some kind of borrowed innocence in the battle ahead.

Airplane hanger 3 stood at the edge of the then brand-new Lahore airport. It was vast, dark and, save for a long table under three hanging lights in the center, entirely empty. Behind the table stood a commanding officer—a dour woman in a brown headscarf—flanked by various customs officers and security guards, all of them men. I approached with the timidity of Oliver Twist going up to the breakfast buffet, my footsteps echoing across the cavernous emptiness like the sound of sarcastic clapping. I spotted the portfolio of my thesis drawings splayed out on the table, its bindings violently ripped open so that all my naked self-portraits lay flat in one neat, mortifying line.

"Good morning!" I said.

"Did you make these?" the lady demanded, ignoring my greeting. She wore a standard issue uniform that had been awkwardly tailored to her expansive curves. Her thin lips were overdrawn in bright red pencil, an impressive attempt at femininity imposed on her otherwise handsome visage.

"Yes," I replied, cowering under her gaze. "Is—is there a problem?"

Her rage flushed deeper than her rouge. "You make these . . . these . . . *vulgarities*!" she said, launching zircons of spit my way. "And ask if there is a *problem*?! Don't you have any shame in your blood? Any decency? Any honor?"

The guard beside her smirked at me, the kind of self-satisfied way schoolchildren do when the class favorite is finally humiliated by the teacher.

"The project was for my final exams," I began. "It involved—"

"Immoral! Un-Islamic! Shameless! Indecent!"

The judgments shot out faster than I could duck them. She went on for quite a bit actually, saying how there could be charges against me for this kind of lewdness, how my school, nay, the very *country's* reputation had been put at immeasurable risk by my wanton disregard of modesty, how the indecency of exploiting a woman's body like this was the very pinnacle of immoral—

"I'm sorry," I interjected. "Perhaps it's just the sound of the airplanes, but I thought I heard you say . . . pictures of women?"

She was not used to interruptions, and in her surprised silence a realization dawned on me with the golden fluidity of a happy sunrise.

"You couldn't think," I asked, with as much incredulity as one can muster in an airline hangar, "that *these* are drawings of *women*?" I gestured at the page closest to us, on which I had drawn two mangoes floating over my bare chest as South Asian symbols for breast tissue. She looked radiantly uncomfortable as she processed the balance of our situation, and for a single moment I felt pity for her, but that was quickly replaced with a warm sense of vengeful elation.

"My thesis was on being *fat*. These"—I pointed at the orchard of breasts laid out on the table—"are drawings of my own body. Anatomical self-portraits, if you will."

"Self . . . portraits?" she repeated in a strained voice, obviously trying to think of some way to wrestle back her rapidly departing high horse. "But . . . but there isn't even a face in some of them. That one just has mangoes!"

"Mmmm," I said. "The project was about gluttony in the South Asian wedding, so I thought I'd use food. You know, with *all* the wasted catering and the ornate outfits, it's quite a commentary on the greed in our culture, don't you see?"

She did not.

"Besides, you'd be surprised how difficult it is to just walk up to random fat men and ask to draw their chests, so I thought I'd use myself as a, well, model. So to speak. I've lost a bit of weight since then," I added, as the group leaned over to study a drawing of my breasts as feuding in-laws. "Mostly cardio but with some free weights every other day. It's the calorie deficit that really does the trick."

The tribunal stared back at me, slack-jawed.

"Can you see that?" I went on, correctly sensing I'd lose my advantage if I stopped speaking. "That dark patch over there? That's my facial hair. And here, see? That's my chest hair. Now, how many women do you know with hairy nipples?"

She declined to say.

"OK," I conceded. "Perhaps I could have made them slightly hairier in retrospect, but it *was* a very stressful time before the exams, and underarm hair is really a very personal grooming—"

"What were you thinking?!"

I winced, but she was shouting at the smirking subordinate. It was obvious from his crushed expression that he thought his morning would turn out rather differently. "You *moron*! You bring this child's drawings up on serious charges and can't even tell the difference between a man and a woman's body? *Jahil!* Imbecile! Cretin!"

She slowly backed away from the table as she spat out fresh insults so that by the time she ordered the men to release my work, she was already running through the far exit. I grabbed my drawings and hurried back to my car, grateful perhaps for the first time ever for both my tits.

"One more month," I muttered to myself on the drive home. "Just one more month."

Chapter 8

OH . . . CANADA?

ROBIN WILLIAMS ONCE DESCRIBED CANADA as "a loft apartment over a really big party"—a phrase that lives on the corner of Cruelty and Truth where I one day intend to own a summer home. I'd never visited Canada before moving there for freshman year, and frankly, most of my prior knowledge was gleaned from Margaret Atwood novels and an early obsession with Celine Dion's wedding tiara. Canada, and particularly her Euro-lite daughter Montreal, is a kind, welcoming place, but not exactly where I had planned to land on the American continent.

My own admissions cycle was a fiasco that took twelve years and three doses of magic mushrooms to process, but I comforted myself by repeating that at least I'd made it to a good college abroad in the same city as Jibran, one that not only accepted difference but celebrated it.

Those first weeks of living in Montreal felt like taking a deep breath after a long underwater swim. The city looked gray from inside the taxi on my way to my dorms, but the closer we got toward the college's downtown campus, the more I saw the charming approximation of a French town in the arctic circle that everyone had been raving about. I enrolled in courses on moral philosophy and gender studies, lived in a Hilton the school had converted into a dorm, and, perhaps best of all, was assigned my own bathroom with an attached hair dryer. On the first day of class I walked through the fall frost holding a latte in a disposable cup like a heroine on a TV show. In the evenings I sat with a gamut of new friends from all over the world chatting over plastic take-out containers of pad thai and green curry. Jibran had already been living in Montreal for a year by then and took me for tours of the city with the authority of a dowager duchess showing off her estate to visiting cousins. My parents came to drop me off at college, and I had waited for them to text me from Pakistan before daring to venture out to any gay clubs (bless the Canadian drinking age of eighteen), lest they ran into me on a street downtown dangling from a dildo.

Jibran and I spent a whole week bickering over the right outfit for my debut onto the gay stage, debating which shirt went with which jacket or which shoes made me look both approachable and aloof. I settled on an old favorite, a type of T-shirt we'd nicknamed the "boob hider" because of the band of contrasting fabric that ran across at nipple level that cast the pleasing illusion of flatness on an otherwise bumpy landscape. Sadly, digital photographs have since confirmed that any camouflage was entirely delusional; turns out the band didn't hide my boobs so much as give them a plinth to rest on. I'm slightly embarrassed to admit it wasn't until a decade later that I finally correlated my late high school weight loss with the act of coming out to my friends. That ridding yourself of one weight might also help lighten another still feels too cliche a thought to be true. I just assumed it was because I stopped eating cake every single day, which, admittedly, is also fair.

Now here I was: abroad, single, thinner if not thin. I would find my perfect boyfriend and live my perfect life. Finally, away from the dust and dirt and discrimination of the Islamic Republic, I could be myself.

I secretly hoped that my first time entering a gay club would be like the crescendo of *Hello, Dolly!*: me, feathered and besequinned, descending an ornate gold staircase as a choir of adoring gays sang, "It's so nice to have you back where you belong!" in warm, welcoming baritones. That I didn't wear sequins was only the first disappointment of the evening.

I scanned the crowd outside the club as we crossed a cobblestoned street in the gay village, the words to "Some Enchanted Evening" playing on a loop inside my head despite the faint dull thumps of bass coming from inside the building.

"Are you excited?" Jibran asked me as we took our place in line behind a man in a latex bodysuit. "Just breathe," he added when he saw my face. "It's going to be fun!"

"Nice T-shirt," the bouncer said as he stamped my hand with the club's rooster insignia. The entrance led us through a series of narrow hallways where packs of sleeveless steroids silently stalked the darkened corners of a vast subterranean labyrinth. The clubs entrance reeked of bleach and sweat, its painted black walls nearly entirely covered by a decade's worth of posters and fliers: SAFE SEX! USE A CONDOM! DIGNITY WITH HIV! DRAG BINGO!

Most of the messaging about gay sex in the early 2000s—a world well before the miracle HIV-prevention drug PrEP or campaigns like Undetectable=Untransmittable—revolved around the pervasive but persuasive fear of contracting HIV. Any mention of gay intimacy in the popular imagination was nearly always entwined with a militantly antiseptic enforcement of safe sex. Most gay men like me, who came of age after the worst of the AIDS crisis but before the peace of mind of PrEP, internalized these warnings as gospel.

Dangerous.

Not everyone my age shared this sense of impending infection. My new coterie of straight girlfriends, for example, would often brag over our Sunday brunches about their latest sexual conquests (one realizes quickly that college kids only ever talk about drugs or sex, unless they have access to neither, in which case they talk about Foucault) and I was shocked by their cavalier attitudes about not using condoms.

"Aren't you afraid?" I asked, already imagining their future of plasma tests and T-cell counts.

"Why?" the girls would reply, utterly unbothered. "I'm on the pill."

Moments like these confirmed that we lived in different realities, they and I. While straight people used condoms to prevent life, gay men used them to avoid death. Well-meaning as the safety campaigns were, they often ignored the pressing stigma they enforced on the psyche of generations of gay men who were told daily that their sex—and usually *only* their sex—was inherently unsafe, essentially dirty, and inevitably lethal.

Most of the world views gayness, particularly male gayness, as a sex act before it is anything else. That's wrong for a variety of reasons, only the third of which is that if a boy thinks of himself as gay, particularly as a young child, it probably isn't because he's participated in a sex act, but because he has experienced romantic feelings for another male. The distinction might seem small to you, but it makes the difference between life and death. Despite my best efforts, sex itself did not constitute a major wedge of my cream-pie chart, but my identity as a gay man did. What was the difference? Even if I ignored my history with Zariyan and the pervasiveness of secret homosexual sex acts in places like Pakistan, a part of me knew intrinsically that gay men were not simply men who slept with other men, but men who fell *in love* with other men. I wanted a whole life, not a single night.

Jibran and I walked past a large plastic replica of Michelangelo's *David* wearing a leather harness and entered a massive dance hall, its basilican proportions soaring up to a firmament of twinkling disco balls. Hundreds of sweaty men writhed on a huge, checkered dance floor in the center of the room, all of them monotonously shirtless and unforgivably chiseled. The ones who looked most like porn stars were already dancing on the raised platforms to a remix of the latest Britney song.

"That actually *is* a porn star," Jibran confirmed when I pointed to a particularly offensive set of abs to our right, and we squealed out together in voyeuristic joy that this was now our glamorous new reality.

After an uneventful hour of awkward eye contact with strangers and sipping cosmos, Jibran suggested we hunt separately and before I could reply he was already chatting to a handsome redhead across the bar. I envied his natural ease with strangers, the currency of gay socializing.

I walked over to a prominent corner of the bar and arranged myself on a red pleather stool in what I hoped was a masculine sprawl but probably looked like incontinence. I wasn't alone. Nearly every man was performing in some kind of way and only a conspicuous handful of us weren't shirtless. We—fellow devotees of the Order of the Sisters of Perpetual Modesty—lurked in the darkness like deep sea creatures waiting for passing prey to float down. An hour later Jibran found me hiding next to a vending machine for condoms, his T-shirt already drenched in sweat from dancing to "Barbie Girl."

"Girl," he said, grabbing my hand and dragging me into the mass of sweaty dancers, "it's time to have some fun!" ABBA came on and there was a collective shriek as a burst of sparkling confetti exploded over the dance floor. More half-naked bodies joined the crowd and, just as I let my guard down, I felt a calloused hand slide up my shirt and stroke my left boob.

"HOW DARE YOU!" I screamed, clutching my hemline. I looked down to see a cute brunette with plucked eyebrows, big arms, and small calves gyrating into my hips.

"Where are you from, handsome?" he asked me.

"Pakistan," I said, smiling tentatively.

"Mmm," he growled in my ear. "I love Arab men."

"I'm not actually Arab," I said.

"What?" he shouted over the drum beat to a Cher song.

I repeated myself but something about the way he slurred "I lurve Arab cock . . ." suggested he hadn't heard me.

2004 was an ambivalent time for gayness in mainstream Western culture. *Will & Grace* was on television (always meant for a straight audience), but saying "That's so gay" was still an entirely acceptable way to denigrate something. American legislative bodies were passing an extraordinary number of laws to limit gay people's roles in public life and space. I remember seeing an ad on TV that began with two young men looking at each other in a school hallway like secret lovers. One nods and the other surreptitiously follows him into an abandoned corridor and you think, *OMG they're gonna do it!* They inch closer and closer to each other, lips near enough to touch, until one boy abruptly whips out a pack of cigarettes from his jeans.

"Are they gay?" the narrator asks in a menacing tenor as the two boys take turns lighting their cigarettes. "Or are they smoking? Remember . . . it's *gay* to smoke."

I came out to my dormmates on the first day I arrived in Montreal, naively assuming that as a foreigner from Pakistan I was merely catching up with everybody else's sexual emancipation. Surely these Western kids, who'd grown up with proms, malls, and multiplexes, were light years ahead of me. Later that day I came back from a poster sale in the quad to find a note scrawled on my room door: *Faggot*. My parents were following me from the elevator, so I quickly wiped the message off with the cuff of my sleeve and pretended nothing had happened. The sense of panic was all too familiar. My ears throbbed, my vision narrowed, my chest tightened. It took me some hours to remind myself that I was not wrong here. Here, in Canada in 2003,

I was legal. I was, technically, safe. Within months these thoughts were joined by the depressing realization that in a college dorm of six hundred (mostly white) students, I was the only one I knew who was out. In retrospect, this was the first crack in my shaky assumption that gayness was an exclusively Western and entirely white construct, but I tried not to think about it too much for the rest of my sexless year in Montreal. Eventually a smattering of others did come out of the closeted woodwork, but I looked at them as one would at soldiers arriving late to a battle I'd been fighting alone for months.

It wasn't simply my peers' apparent reticence about their sexuality that made me feel like an outsider in the gay world abroad. It was also that everyone in the clubs looked like another white clone soldier in an army of Botox and biceps, and in the days before apps like Grindr made hookups easier, the general impression was that to meet any man I would have to rely on the awkward art of cruising. Pathologically trained by Lahori drawing room etiquette to avoid unsolicited conversation, let alone aggressive eye contact, I was as good at cruising as I was at hockey, not least because, disarmed of wit and words, my body was left to do most of the talking.

Despite my weight loss, my body and I were never far away from calling lawyers to start divorce proceedings. I still dressed in oversize clothes, habitually tugging at my chest to create the illusion that it was the fabric and not my tits that bulged, while the rest of me I hid behind a slew of well-structured jackets and voluminous scarves. Overdressed but under-verbal, I spent the next several months going to gay clubs with Jibran on the weekends only to leave alone every night feeling like the homely vicar's daughter at a Jane Austen ball.

The clubs didn't just feel intimidating, they felt hostile, angrily insistent on a manicured homogeneity of which I was quite literally incapable. Plus—and I don't care how many times soap ads tell me to love my body—there was no way I was going shirtless in a room of five hundred strangers whose closest adult relationship was with a pair of fifty-pound dumbbells and a box of prescription-strength laxatives.

Jibran, poor thing, patiently listened to me complain over our weekly brunches until he eventually suggested I try online dating. He'd been on several dates by then, which was enough to make him my sexpert. We sat together at a Tim Hortons coffee shop to make my first online profile on gay.com, that Wild West of early hookup forums.

Looking for? Love.

No, not love, too needy.

Looking for? An epic smile.

Yes, better!

My first date was with a balding forty-four-year-old white man who was studying to become a priest at a rural seminary school. After dinner we made out in a dark park behind a World War II memorial because the movie we wanted to see was sold out and later he began crying in my armpit about his mother. I had to remind myself on the snowy walk home that my first kiss was actually Zariyan.

It was around eight P.M. or so. I was holding a plate of dinner from the cafeteria when a beer bottle exploded on the wall opposite me, its remnants scattered across the carpeted floor like petals of glass. I followed the debris to the very end of the corridor, where a group of four boys were physically restraining a thrashing blur.

"Faggot!" Spit flew out of his mouth and his eyes bulged maniacally as he struggled to free himself. I recognized him as a short desi Canadian named Ash who lived two floors down.

"FUCKING FAGGOT!" he screamed. Ash managed to pull one hand free and flung an empty vodka bottle at me, this one landing much closer.

"Sorry!" one of his friends shouted my way, still struggling to hold the now thankfully empty-handed Ash from charging. "He's just high, man! Ignore him!"

"Fuck off HOME!" Ash screamed. His voice was unnaturally high, crackling with Napoleonic rage. "Fucking faggot!"

I casually leaned against the wall to watch this homophobic *tableau vivant* play out as I ate my poutine, determined to demonstrate I didn't care. By now others had come out of their rooms to see what the commotion was about, and his friends continued shouting out apologies. Eventually, with the help of two linebackers, the group dragged Ash behind a locked door. An hour later there was a knock on my door.

"I *just* heard what happened!" The RA sounded genuinely disturbed.

"Oh my God, what happened?" I asked, already anticipating a dorm room love triangle.

"To *you*!" she said incredulously. "You were *attacked* tonight!"

"Attacked?" I said, trying to understand what she meant. "Oh, you mean the *bottle*! No, no, no. Nothing actually happened."

"Are you OK? Are you sure you're not injured?"

"Yeah, I'm fine!" I said, a little embarrassed by all the fuss she was making. "It's OK!"

"No," she insisted. "It's not OK. Do you want to press charges? We can, you know. I can't *believe* someone would say something like that to you. I'm so sorry."

I declined to press any charges, but the next day she emailed me to say that Ash had been summoned to the dean's office for a suspension hearing. I felt an unfamiliar sense of flattery that the university would consider my well-being such a priority for something as routine as a homophobic slur. I had, after all, suffered far worse than an angry inchling armed with bottles. Many weeks later I was out in the polar vortex of downtown Montreal when Ash rushed up to me from across a snow drift.

"Hey, man," he said, avoiding my eyes. "Just wanted to say . . . well, acid . . . ya know? It's a bitch. But listen, bro, I got nothin' but mad respect for you, bro, being gay from Pakistan? I mean, mad respect."

"Yes," I replied. "Clearly."

The rest of freshman year unfolded without incident. I made a large group of friends and took classes on African art, Latin American politics, and Greek philosophy, and within months Montreal felt like home. But I couldn't shake a growing feeling of discontent, ever aware that my relationship with Canada was meant to be an affair and not a marriage. That spring break I took advantage of my US tourist visa and flew to New York City with friends. We stayed in a ratty hotel near Times Square, and I spent most of the week and all my money ricocheting from one Broadway show to another, counting down the days until I'd be forced to leave this nirvana of musicals for the comparatively boring sanity of the maple leaf matron. It was during one of those Broadway shows, a Wednesday performance of *Rent*, that I silently made the decision to do everything I could to move to New York City.

I had reasons. For one, Montreal is an icy tundra for most of the year; for another, Quebecois French is an altogether unmanageable tongue to master in under eight months. But mostly I wanted to leave because I felt that gayness itself emanated from the construct that is New York City, a spell echoed in every queer history book and gay movie trope I studied so voraciously at school. Like my father's attachment to Lahore, I too felt a primordial pull to a city of my ancestors, except mine were less old courtiers than young queens. I heard them whisper to me before sleep, calling me home to the gridded chaos where generations of other queer people had lived and loved, a place where our iridescence had lit a magical flame so bright that no amount of bigotry could extinguish it. The legacy of our queer ancestors lives on in places like New York still, enshrined in the treasure of plays, books, paintings, songs, art, and longing that will remain signposts to dignity for new refugees for years to come.

I applied to NYU with an essay on how I handled my family's homophobia growing up and sent in the application without telling anyone. After term ended, Noor and I embarked on a glorious three-week journey through Italy on a budget trip we'd deliberately modeled on a grand tour of nineteenth-century dandies had they been forced to stay in youth hostels. He was by my side at the internet café in Florence when I received the email congratulating me on my acceptance into NYU and we jumped around the piazza screaming for fifteen minutes until a police officer finally asked us to stop. By the following autumn I was moving into my new dorms, convinced that there, on the crossroads of the Villages East and West and a stone's throw from the Stonewall Inn, I would find authenticity. There, I would have a boyfriend. There my life could finally begin.

Chapter 9

FREEDOM FRIES

Are you a terrorist?
Of course not. Officer Stuart, is it?

You call me sir and only sir. Do you understand that?
Yes, sir.

Good. Now let's try that again. Are you a terrorist?
No, sir.

Have you been to Afganeestan in the last decade?
No, sir.

What about Eyeran?
No, sir.

Are you sure?
Yes, sir.

What about Eyerack?
No, sir.

Have you been trained or provided training at terrorist camps in the past three months?
No, sir.

Have you attended any religious gatherings at a mosque in the last three months?
No, sir.

Do you know how to make a bomb?
No, sir.

What are your views on the United States?
Good, sir.

To be a Muslim living in America from 2001 onward has required the constant performance of gratitude. Thank you, my smile was expected to convey, thank you for letting me in, thank you for giving me the benefit of the doubt, thank you for not hating me on sight. That's so Freedom of you.

Whenever we study periods of great global turmoil, it is often with a comforting sense of closure. The rise of virulent nationalism and fascists in Europe in the early twentieth century, for instance, is nearly always described in context to their seemingly inevitable defeat. A neat, tidy little package wrapped up in a battered but beautiful bow. One of the consequences of learning history this way is that we expect real world events to have clear-cut beginnings and finite endings, but the truth of lived experience is often far less linear than historians care to admit. When they were still alive, I used to ask my mother's parents questions about their youth in the 1930s and '40s, a period as romantic in my imagination as black-and-white movies like *Casablanca*.

What was life like before TV? Did everyone use gramophones?
Did you actually see Nazi planes whizzing over your houses? What
do you mean there were no Germans in the Himalayas? You didn't
have indoor toilets? What's an outhouse?

Whenever my grandmother spoke about the partition of India in
1947—the painful cleaving that remains the foundational trauma of
modern South Asia—it was never with the level of drama I expected.
There were no slow hikes over mountain ranges to escape chasing
armies or last-minute dashes across barbed-wire borders while clutching fake passports.

"We weren't in *The Sound of Music*, you know," she said, amused
at my frustration that her war stories weren't sufficiently traumatic,
and I watched as she resumed brushing her impossibly long hair. Most
of the time she kept her tresses in a loosely knotted braid so long that
it grazed the backs of her knees, but on rare occasions, like this, I
could see it open and free in all its a Pre-Raphaelite glory, tumbling
down in soft, thick auburn waves that had not been cut for over sixty
years. She once told me she was the inspiration for Rapunzel; any
child would have believed her.

"It wasn't so easy to communicate back then," she went on,
holding her ends up high as she jabbed at the tangles with a wide-
toothed comb. "You have to understand it was all one country. There
was no Pakistan, no India, no Bangladesh. It was all just India. So
when we left our house in Srinagar to come to Lahore for a visit,
we had no idea, none at all, that we'd never go back home again.
Life," she added, flinging her detangled mane over her shoulder in a
graceful swoop, "can change quite suddenly." Her fingers danced as
she quickly knotted her locks into a three-foot braid. "One moment
life is one way, and the next . . . well." She looked sad, as she often
did when she spoke of her childhood. "Anyway, never mind these
things. Tell me: What can I make my little prince to eat, huh? Don't

be silly! Of course you're hungry. All children are hungry. Here, have some cake."

The prospect that immovable things like countries could simply disappear in an instant felt more bone-chilling to me than all the stories of blood and gore we were taught at school. As a child, I still didn't quite understand how my grandparents—wise, well-read, and worldly as they were—couldn't have predicted what my history books laid out in such a clear timeline. But as anyone who has lived in New York City for longer than five art movements knows, history is a story that only happens in retrospect. The present is just a series of moments strung together with hope and cake.

Despite my immigrant aspirations (or perhaps because of them), international travel to anywhere in the world after 2001 made me very uncomfortable. Pakistani citizens need a visa to so much as look at another country on the map, and the process of acquiring one is long and, I suspect, deliberately humiliating. The applications require months of preplanning, reams of financial statements, stacks of recommendations, and a legion of prepaid flight tickets, including hotel bookings, blood tests, chest X-rays, and assurances from schools, colleagues, banks, and loved ones confirming that you have any reason to travel at all. Student visas had a higher burden of proof. Even with a visa, a Pakistani passport was enough to trigger an entirely separate array of inquisitions at airports the world over. Unsurprisingly, the United States excelled at this. It only took an acid-green flash of my passport for immigration officers to give me the kind of exasperated groan usually reserved for that one uninvited guest dangerously close to creating a scene at your catered sit-down dinner for twelve.

Do you have any bruises on your legs from combat training?
No, sir.

Show me.
Here, sir?

Yes. OK, that's enough. Do you know how to operate a plane?
No, sir.

Have you or anyone you know taken lessons in how to fly a plane?
No, sir.

NSEERS began in the United States in 2002. I'd like to say you're forgiven for not knowing from its name that the National Security Entry-Exit Registration System was a Muslim-specific program, but I'm not that generous a person. Like thousands of others, I only found out because I had to.

"Found out" implies there was something to look for, but NSEERS existed more like rumor back then. There was no televised declaration, no press release, no woke internet thread to guide you through being openly racially profiled in the permissive madness that overtook America after 9/11. Only whispers: An international student not allowed back into the States after leaving the country for spring break; an elderly couple separated at the airport and deported back on different flights; thirty-hour plane journeys followed by six-hour interrogations, never certain if you'll be able to leave the airport at all.

I was so envious of those around me with the privilege of a Western passport, and angry at the undeserved ease with which they floated above a system specifically designed to curtail my own freedom of movement so effectively. I promised myself that one day I too would have an American passport. *Then I'll be free. Then*, I reasoned, *I'll finally belong here.*

The only upside of the United States–led invasions of Iraq and Afghanistan (bright move, you must be so proud), was that I began to see a lot more people on American TV who looked like me. The bad news was they all played terrorists. The only thing we did know for certain at the time was that if you were a Muslim male in the US between the ages of twelve and eighty, gay or otherwise, you were under surveillance with a presumption of guilt and you had no right to complain about it, because Freedom.

What's the password for your computer?
Shall I open it for you, sir?

Don't you understand plain English? What. Is. The. Password?
Dolly Levi. Sir.

Hand the computer to us and wait until you are called. What's that?
It's my diary, sir.

Hand that over too.
Yes, sir.

July 4, 2008, was a date so monumental that it was committed to my mitochondrial memory, like a birthday or goal weight or the precise number of drops of belladonna it takes to kill someone. It marked the exact day my US student visa would end, and with it, my life in America. I used to call it Dependence Day, and it was why I felt like a tub of yogurt on the perpetual precipice of expiration throughout college.

The value of living in a country full of people who don't look like you is that it strips you of the presumption of belonging. My move

to North America did not give me a culture shock in the real sense of
the term; colonialism, privilege, and queerness meant that I related to
Western culture to the point where I identified most of it as my own.
That did not, I discovered, translate into how I was seen by others.
I'd spent years in Pakistan being ridiculed as an anglicized English
speaker, uncomfortable in the native language and a traitor to my
culture. But now I was anointed a Pakistani in the West, forced to
defend a belonging I'd not yet experienced.

Canada aspired to egalitarianism in both its politics and culture,
and being Pakistani there never felt remotely dangerous because,
after all, everyone was from somewhere. But that sense of welcoming
apathy changed the second I moved to the United States, where the
particularly American obsession with race is immediately obvious and
brutally enforced. I was now a brown-skinned Muslim male before
I was anything else. Yet another visitor from the land of enemies to
be treated with suspicion if not outright hostility. Nowhere was this
more obvious than at border control.

The NSEERS questioning room at JFK airport looked like an
informal jail for first time offenders at the UN, but it smelled much
worse. Inside, rows of collapsible chairs faced a raised stage where
uniformed officers sat in bored judgment as dozens of trembling
passengers cowered before them like supplicants. The bone-gray walls
were decorated with posters of bald eagles staring aggressively at the
US flag and at least one cross-eyed portrait of Bush the Younger. The
officers talked loudly to each other—inane things like what they ate
for dinner or the next shift break—as if the room wasn't crowded with
people but it always was: young families, crying kids, tired mothers,
worried students, exhausted grandparents, anxious businessmen,
not one of them white and all peering with deferential energy at the
guards to prove somehow that they weren't *those* kinds of Muslims.
One by one the guards would shout out a mangled name and tut
impatiently as a passenger struggled to reach the kiosks with their

life's paperwork. Sometimes the process took a spritely three hours, other times it took over nine. Either way, you hoped whoever was interviewing you was in a good mood.

I flew back to Lahore over my first winter break at NYU to attend my middle sister's wedding (same rain, different tent) and was delayed in getting back to school by three days. I'd emailed my advisor, who said it wouldn't be an issue, but the red-haired officer at JFK scanning my documents did not agree.

"How do we even know you're still enrolled?" His thick Long Island accent couldn't hide the sibilant *s*, and I felt an involuntary wave of relief sweep over me that I was with a fellow gay man. "We have no *proof*. You could've been expelled by now. You got any *proof* from them you are still *allowed* to be in class? No, not your schedule! I swear to God, these *people* . . ." He looked at his companion in exasperation. "No! Do you have a letter from the school?"

I did not.

"Jeez!" he hissed loudly. "You think you can just walk in here whenever you like, huh? Like it's *your* country."

He told me I was going to be sent back to Pakistan on the next flight home and flung my paperwork into a red file on the desk with a theatrical sweep. "I suggest you stop talking until someone comes to get you," he said when I tried to argue. I slunk back to my seat as the entire room watched me in silent pity. Other travelers were called up, questioned, and released until, four hours later, only I remained. I waited, alternating between quiet tears and stony desolation. The officers had changed shifts by then.

"Haven't you been called yet?" a younger woman asked me as she entered the room.

"I was," I said, hurrying up to her. "But the officer before you said there was an issue." I explained my predicament.

"Redhead?" she asked with a smirk as she settled into her chair. I nodded, still fighting back the tears that refused to cooperate. She leaned over and took my paperwork from the red file beside her. "Let's see, what was the problem?"

"He said there was no proof I was still enrolled at the school."

"Because you missed three days?"

I nodded.

"Yeah." She shook her head. "Benny's been in a bad mood all week."

The name didn't suit him. "Benny" made him sound saccharine, like a happy, winsome debutant who wore pastel linen dresses and baked apricot pies. The man who'd harassed me looked like a pit bull called something meaty like Bertha. Yes, Bertha the duplicitous pit bull. In a musical he would appear in villainous drag at the end of the first act wearing a leather—

"Hello?"

"Yes." I snapped back to the florescent hellscape. "Yes, sorry. It's . . . it's been a long day."

She shot me grimace-laced smile, and I felt such gratitude for even that small act of compassion.

"Listen," she said. "You're *fine*. Go on, have a great semester." She stamped my passport with a loud thwack as if to confirm the finality of her mercy and handed it back to me with a grin. I walked out to the baggage claim in a daze, my bags the sole suitcases left in the hall. It wasn't until I opened my apartment door that I let myself feel how truly close I came to losing everything. The subsequent panic attack didn't end for weeks.

Muslims also had to register with NSEERS before leaving the country, a fact I discovered only because a boy from the Academy was deported back to Pakistan for forgetting to do so. If you had the misfortune of living near an airport that didn't have a NSEERS office, well, that was on you. Not that they ever made those rooms easy to find. The one at JFK was next to a utility closet.

For the next eight years I spent a lot of time in that room languishing under homophobic lighting, every mandatory interrogation another reminder of just how firmly entrenched the institutional hostility against me was in Bush's America.

What are you studying at college?
Fine art studies. Sir.

What's that?
It's the history of art, sir.

Why?
Well, I suppose someone had to write it down. Sir.

I chose to major in art history at college because I secretly hoped all my classes would be as life changing as Julia Roberts's in *Mona Lisa Smile*. But there were other reasons too, reasons that grew tenuously out of family roots that burrowed far deeper than my long name would let me forget.

I was nine the first time my father took me to the painting galleries in the Royal Fort of Lahore, a large and imposing Mughal-era palace that still sits in regal dishevelment at the center of the Old City. It retains some remnants of its glorious past—marble fountains, perforated stone walls, a mirrored hall that turns a flame into a firmament—but age and men have stripped the palace down to its bare brick facing. The painting gallery was housed in an abandoned set of rooms that used to be the apartments for a dowager queen, a dark, dusty, and decrepit chamber that, like so many of my great-aunts, stubbornly clung to a past glory despite decades of neglect.

A spectacular collection of oil paintings lined the walls, mostly portraits of Sikh royals dripping in pearls and dotted with diamonds, that were painted in the style of European masters. The centerpiece of the collection was a monumentally large panoramic painting, as wide as the hall itself and so tall that it touched the vaulted ceiling, which depicted the turbaned faces and bejeweled bodies of each of many members of the nineteenth-century court of Lahore in their full regalia.

"That man over there," my father said, pointing at the painting, "is our ancestor." I followed his finger through the crowds on the canvas to find an old man sitting on a plinth under a marble arch. He had a rounded nose and a long white beard and wore an ornate embroidered outfit that accentuated a magnificent pair of tits. If not for his robes, I thought to myself, he could pass for any of the uncles I saw at family lunches sitting in the shade and arguing about politics. I recognized my aunt's thick eyebrows, my great uncle's bulbous nose, *khala* Boob's bustline. And, as I studied those flicks of paint made centuries ago by a forgotten Hungarian painter, I was momentarily shocked to recognize an infinitesimal part of myself frozen in time.

There was pride in my father's eyes as he explained the painting to me, as if in bringing me to see it he had now fulfilled an old promise to a watchful ghost. I thought of the generations of fathers and sons that formed a biological chain between the man in the painting and me. Did they ever feel as lonely as I did? Were any of them effeminate and gay? What was my role in this chorus line? Was I expected to bring my son here one day? I knew even then I didn't want a wife and so, presumably, would not have kids. What would happen when I couldn't live up to the most basic form of genetic replication to which my very existence in front of this painting was a testament? Would I still be part of a chain? A family?

Studying art history at college felt like a fulfillment of an unspoken familial duty, a merger of interests to compensate for whatever I imagined my father lost because his only son was gay. It would take a long time to realize that I didn't owe compensation for the fact of me to anyone, even our ancestors.

Art history was also a way for me to study painting without admitting that I wanted to actually make art myself. Art history served as an intellectual disguise, a respectable, heterosexual-adjacent field for the artistically inclined, not unlike architecture, perfect for the creative soul too scared to admit to the world or themselves that what they really wanted to be was a swishy fashion designer.

NYU's curriculum began with Introduction to Western Art, which is essentially another way of saying Introduction to White People's Art. It's better to quickly identify the implicit racial bias in subjects that purport to be historical fact in American colleges, since that way you're not left confused as to why Mayan or modernist Mexican art is not included in what I naively assumed was a mostly geographical classification. I didn't mind at the time because, at least for me, art history was also my quickest door into the secret history of gay male creation through the ages. (It only takes a glance at the Sistine Chapel to realize Michelangelo had a pec fetish and very low self-esteem.)

It was in those dark lecture halls, staring wide-eyed at the brightly colored slides of works by Praxiteles, Caravaggio, and Marsden Hartley, that I learned tales of legendary gay couples through history: Achilles and Patroclus, Alexander and Hephaestion, Khnumhotep and Niankhkhnum, Hadrian and Antinous, Gilgamesh and Enkidu, mythical stories that were all the proof I needed that gay love—not simply the act of homosexual sex, but actual deified love—is as old as humanity itself. What most of you are taught through Disney, some of us still learn through stone tablets.

Or porn.

We were well into our studies of Hellenic art when the movie *Alexander* came out, a flop epic starring an underrated Colin Farrell with Angelina Jolie as his mother. When the aged professor brought up the film as a sign of Alexander's enduring legacy throughout history, a student from Greece raised his hand.

"I don't like that they made it seem he was gay," he said tersely. "It's an *insult* to my whole country."

The only insult here is that you only have one long eyebrow, I wanted to say, *but you don't see me being an ass about it.* Alexander may have lived in lands that were now Greece, but he is supposed to have died in what is today Pakistan, and I felt as much right to claim him as the other guy did. More even, given the boy's demonstrable aversion to tweezers.

Have you taken part in any protests in America?
No, sir.

Are you sure? Nothing about the war?
No, sir.

You know we'll find out if you have right?
Yes, sir.

If enough people remind you that you don't belong, eventually you start believing it yourself. "Muslim," "Islam," and "Terror" were now woven into a knot of American fear, every other news story yet another reminder how quickly the old-world order was changing. The image of America I had worshipped for so long from afar—a hodgepodge of political progression, cultural freedom, and, at its core, a welcoming neutrality rooted in meritocratic fairness—felt on good days like a shoddy illusion and on bad days like a deliberate lie. It was painful to find that the United States was a white, Christian country before it was anything else, including sane. For all the American condescension I heard at Islam's outsize role in Muslim societies, I couldn't help but notice that American money too had God's name on it, here too was blasphemy a threat, and here too were founding fathers treated like infallible prophets, a collection of convenient corpses to be routinely reanimated whenever the majority felt threatened.

Having spent years plotting to escape the limits that state-sponsored religion exerted on my personal life in Pakistan, the irony of being told to carry my Muslim card this close to the Stonewall Inn was infuriating.

As an antidote, I tried out for college plays so I could fulfill my Patti LuPone fantasy. This didn't go well for many reasons, one of which was I had no theatrical training whatsoever. The Academy didn't really have a dedicated drama department (aside from a trio of divorced teachers who had affairs with each other), and while I'd assumed there would be some light competition for roles in plays at NYU, absolutely nothing had equipped me to do battle with neurotic musical theatre majors driven by paternal disappointment and a four-octave range.

I focused instead on getting laid, and in that effort, I pledged the first class of a new gay fraternity being formed on campus ("NYU . . . even our frats are gay"). Most of the men I met there were lovely, but I quickly realized our bonds were mostly based on a shared experience of being gay, and while that was true, what was truer was that our bond was predicated on being gay *in America*. I was inside their lived gay experience, but they were not, at the end of it all, invested in mine. Although, in fairness, manboobs aren't exactly a universal experience.

"Your chest isn't even that bad," a young Argentinian told me one night as we shared a postcoital cigarette. We'd met online, and after a brief conversation (it took every ounce of my strength to not to quote *Evita*), he snuck into my dorm room at four A.M. for my first true sexual experience abroad. He was tender and rough and groaned in carnal pleasure when I grabbed him by his throat and thrust inside him. Afterward he'd asked me why I had kept my shirt on during sex, and with the honesty postcoital conversation usually inspires in men, I told him the truth about the burden of my boobs.

"But you look great," he assured me.

I listened without hearing, still convinced I'd tricked rather than attracted this man into bed. His chest was square and muscular, I noticed, the lean lines of his body undulating in all the ways porn and art had taught me a beautiful male body should. From the ropes of muscle on his bronzed forearms to the way his broad back narrowed into an etched waist, the whole of him looked like a statue lifted directly from a Roman villa. After he kissed me goodbye, I marveled at how someone who looked like him could possibly like someone who looked like me, casually slicing open the wounds in my self-esteem for no other reason than habit. I woke up the next morning in a blind panic: What if the condom had broken? What if he was HIV positive? What if I die?

This manic morning madness would become a postsex ritual for years to come until the advent of PrEP. Hours spent online hunting for a partner to feel that brief bout of connection, followed almost immediately by twenty-four hours spent convinced that I'd caught something fatal. Logic didn't help. It didn't matter that I knew we hadn't done anything that would risk transmission or that I had maintained a latex forcefield between our skin at all times. The college clinic took at least a week for test results, so I'd search online for free rapid HIV tests in the city, and it wasn't until a nurse would call me from a waiting room crammed with nervous gay men and actually enunciate the word "negative" out loud that I could finally breathe again. On the walk home I'd vow to myself never to meet random men off the internet again. Until the next time. And the next. And the next.

Dangerous.

Aping heterosexual monogamy with a long-term boyfriend seemed the only real way to stay safe, and I took my inability to attract a steady partner in New York as a personal failure, as if the burden of public health rested solely on my personal choices. Eventually, like almost every other gay man I knew, I took for granted that mortal fear was my price for momentary happiness.

I zoomed from diet to diet, trying this, cutting that, adding these, blending those. And while the rest of me contracted and expanded depending on my self-discipline, my manboobs remained stubborn repositories of my humiliation, the two reasons I avoided pool parties, public beaches, vests, changing rooms, Fire Island, and the entire month of July.

Have you ever spoken or written negatively about American government?
No, sir.

Any school papers about US policies or foreign interventions?
No, sir.

Do you know anyone who has?
No, sir.

I added journalism as a major in junior year. The first article we read in Journalism 101 as an example of what great reportage could be was from an issue of *The New Yorker* published shortly after 9/11. It was about a Sikh family who had been the targets of hate crimes by bigots who mistook them for Muslims because of their turbans. It was well-written, crammed with beautiful imagery of sad Sikh men and mournful cascading hair, and topical because in those early days after 9/11 the evening news was replete with stories of Sikh men being harassed all over the country after being mistaken for Muslims. A few were even murdered in cold blood in Texas, ever the overachiever for ignorance.

"We're not Muslims," the Sikhs would plead in TV interviews. "Our community is peaceful. We are *not* Muslims!"

It was OK to say that then, to make sure people knew you weren't the wrong kind of foreigner. In a global journalism class, we were asked to pitch topics that would be of interest to a broad consortium of international newspapers. Some students proposed writing on New York subway etiquette, others on the rising cost of student living. I wanted to write about my experience of having the term "sand n—r" shouted at me by passing motorists three times in the last month, but instead I pitched an article exploring the Muslim registration process at American airports. Few of the Americans at school believed me when I told them I had to register every time I entered or left the country, so I imagined it might be newsworthy to a broader audience. While I anticipated a certain amount of incredulity, perhaps even hoped for a comforting smidge of liberal outrage, what I didn't expect was for my white professor to ask me, "Why do you think *that* is important for the world to know?"

It was one of the few times in my life, outside of meeting Liza Minnelli at an art opening in Manhattan, that I've been rendered truly mute.

"I mean," began a white guy in a beanie to my left. "They're just doing their job, right? Tryin' to keep us safe." Heads around the table nodded. The Lebanese boy in the corner signaled me with look: *Leave it alone, not worth it.*

The ice-cold sense of betrayal oozed down my scalp like a cracked egg. I didn't argue with them about how NSEERS claimed to screen anyone entering the country but only had twenty-five countries on its list, twenty-four of which happened to be Muslim (the twenty-fifth was North Korea, as if *that* flight landed every day). I didn't point out how the program wouldn't catch a terrorist who entered on a different passport, or confront them with the fact that they were, in this self-professed liberal bastion in downtown New York City, actively advocating for racial profiling but weren't yet self-aware enough to know it. The newsstands outside our class were still plastered with explosive photographs of American soldiers smiling with their thumbs up next to prisoners at Abu Ghraib, squalid naked wretches forced to stand in crucified poses, arms hooked up to electric wiring and heads covered by pointed hoods like grubby KKK klansmen. But to be outraged for Muslims was to betray America. There were no innocent people on the other side of this war, merely the shadowy specter of a faceless Enemy. *You are either with us or against us.* So I did what so many people with brown skin and unusual names did during those years: I kept quiet. The growing tragedy of my American emancipation was not simply that my gay promised land had turned against people who looked like me. It was also the hypocrisy of left-leaning white liberals who refused to acknowledge that this was anything but a bureaucratic inconvenience.

I knew what to do, of course. I pitched a story about a famous gay New York nightclub that was closing permanently that weekend, and this was met with approving smiles because now I was performing my part in the play as the gay Muslim being rescued by the West. My assignment got an A minus, next to a scrawled note: "Maybe add more about the struggle of being Muslim in a gay club?"

For context, another student in the course named Tiffany—a blond travesty who smelled like Febreze and majored in acrylic nails—was showered with praise for writing an article about threading, an ancient South Asian grooming technique that Tiffany didn't think existed until she herself discovered it on Fourteenth Street the week earlier.

Are your parents Muslims?
Yes, sir.

Do they hate the United States?
No, sir.

Have they been to the United States?
Yes, sir.

Do you intend to marry a US citizen in order to gain citizenship?
No, sir.

Can you prove that?
Yes, sir.

Really? How?
The United States doesn't recognize gay marriage.

The biggest misconception about coming out is that you only do it once. It would be nice if that were true, if all you had to do was mutter the words "I am gay" before a glitter bomb exploded out of your prostate and the world suddenly reordered itself into a place worthy of your authenticity.

The truth is you never stop coming out because the world never stops asking.

I was twenty-one when I finally came out to my parents. A year before, my middle sister and I had been chatting about why our cat wasn't mating when she asked me point-blank if I was gay. Deliberately ignoring the jump in her mind from sterile cat to gay brother, I decided to tell her the truth. She sat back for a beat calculating something in her head.

"Don't tell Mom and Dad," I said, eyes down. "Not yet."

"I won't," she said, and left to immediately out me to our older sister. My parents called every day while I was away from home (nearly always separately), both to ask after me in a general way and to find an audience for their grievances. For years I listened out of the belief that if I were there for them, they would be there for me when the time came to come out. I had reasons to hope: My family presented themselves to the world as tolerant, forward-thinking, and well-read liberals. They had paintings and wineglasses, so surely homophobic bigotry had no place in our household of books and tarot cards.

I was in Lahore over winter break of my senior year when I opened my planner and wrote the words *Come Out to Parents* like it was a dentist appointment. It had been three years since I'd left for college. Three long, mostly sexless years spent worrying how my family would find out who I really was and what they would do once they did. I prayed that the worst probably, hopefully, wouldn't happen, but I also knew that coming out would test if a parent's love was truly unconditional.

I asked them both to sit down on the living room couch just

after breakfast. "There is something I have been meaning to tell you for a very long time," I began, my heart beating so hard I could see my shirt moving. They looked at each other, and for a split second, I knew they suspected what was coming. I felt dizzy and nauseous, as one does at the top of a very tall, very shaky wooden roller coaster about to nose-dive into a pool of your worst fears.

"I'm gay."

For all the weight they exerted on my soul, the words felt strangely small. In the mute aftermath of my declaration, I closed my eyes to invoke every camp image, comic goddess, and chiseled god that I'd ever worshipped, anything at all to help me keep myself grounded in the knowledge that I was not wrong.

I was not wrong.

After a beat, my father walked over and wrapped me up in a hug.

I wiped away the mist from my eyes to catch a glimpse of my mother over his shoulder, rooted to her seat, radiating disgust. I had memorized a list of dialogues saved from coming-out scenes in movies, and now I put them to use: "It's only love," I said. "You can be sure you're not the only parents out there with a gay son."

"And *that* is supposed to make me feel better?" she said. "I don't even know what to say to you . . ."

Plot twist: She had tons to say! She said I was abhorrent, a scourge, a disappointment in every way a child could be. After googling what "scourge" meant, I reminded her of all the good things I'd accomplished in my life so far, as if the onus was on me to justify the value of my very existence with a well-filled résumé.

"None of that matters anymore," she said. I waited for my father to interrupt her, to defend me in some way, but he remained quiet, and it felt as if he was relying on her to say what he couldn't. I suspect what disturbed her most was not simply the fact of my homosexuality but that in declaring it without shame I had broken something fundamental in her worldview; people like me don't just get to be ourselves and then demand acceptance. Ridiculous! I've found most people consider being asked to confront their bigotry fundamentally unfair, which is one of the reasons I think "tolerance" is a nasty word. We don't need your tolerance; we're not a passing irritant in your otherwise perfect world that should be grateful because you chose out of the goodness of your dark heart not to attack us on sight. Fuck your tolerance. Fix your hate.

My father continued to sit quietly as I listened to my mother vent her anger, silently forgiving every barbed comment and abusive aside as a temporary reaction to a shock. In truth, it was rather cathartic to hear out loud how absurd her objections were.

"In a way you *have* died for me," she said, staring out into the garden like a widow who'd just received a telegram from the war front.

Be prepared for this, Children of the Fae. When you come out to your parents, you may have to be strong enough for the both of you. It may not make sense, but in that awful moment you are the authority figure—the one who has to show reserve, patience, and dignity in the face of a childhood nightmare made real. Terrifying as it is, if you've made it to the point where you are telling your family that you are gay, particularly in places where being queer is illegal, you're doing so because you need them to hear it more than the world needs you to hide it. It helps to remember that whatever you lose after coming out was never really yours to begin with. Knowing that doesn't take the pain of loss away, of course—little does—but it does help to remind ourselves of our own worth, that our love is sacred, our love is worthy, our love is God.

As my mother dug herself deeper into the bedrock of a stony silence, my father hustled me out of the house for coffee.

"She just needs time," he said.

"I know," I said.

That's the other lie, that time heals all wounds. Some people will remain intractable no matter how much time they are given. Others will present a veneer of acceptance that remains conditional on the fact that you never draw attention to yourself, that you remain in the shadows where they can continue loving the illusion of you.

I asked both my parents to sit for portraits a few days after I came out to them. Whatever their reactions had been, it was important to me to memorialize this moment in paint as a witness to my own life. They, perhaps eager to return the household to some sense of polite normalcy, agreed. My father's portrait shows him smiling ruefully and used to hang in my library in Lahore. My mother's painting shows her as she was: impassive, imperious, one thin eyebrow arched high in curdled love. It currently hangs, as most portraits of disapproving mothers should, in a lesbian's living room in Park Slope.

I flew back to New York the next day, a welcome respite for us all. Noor and I were traveling back to JFK together, his face both eager and anxious as I approached him in the Lahore airport departure lounge.

"Are you OK?" he asked. "How did it go?" I waited to conference-call Ayaan and Jibran before relating the events of the last few days to them all.

"I'm so proud of you," Jibran said from Toronto. "So proud!"

"We all are, darling." Ayaan's voice echoed from Boston.

Noor, who could see my face, said nothing but clutched my hand gently, ignoring the glares coming from the mustached cleric sitting opposite us.

For the next twelve years my entire family and I fell into a mutually observed silence about my sexuality. It existed somewhere far, far away in a place they'd never visit. And I, for my part, let it. Tolerance and acceptance are not conjoined twins. Most of the time they never even meet.

Chapter 10

FLORALS FOR SPRING

I BLAME *THE DEVIL WEARS PRADA* for the mostly millennial delusion that merely graduating college would guarantee a glitzy job that would not only pay enough to fund a waterfront apartment and work visa but also keep me glamorously busy until I met the man of my dreams outside a Vinyasa yoga studio in SoHo one sunny spring morning. Things turned out rather differently.

For my final semester at college, my art history advisor encouraged me to take a course titled Artists of the Eighties. It was to be taught by a famous visiting German art historian called Professor Klaus. One had to apply to get into the class, a thrilling pretension that made me feel like one of the students from Donna Tartt's *The Secret History*. The first day of class, twelve girls and I sat around a boardroom table when in walked an ambitiously overweight man of about seventy, wearing a fedora hat and accompanied by a stunningly beautiful male graduate assistant.

Klaus boasted of knowing the artists we were to study personally—all of them now living legends in their own right—by virtue of the fact that he was a friend of Andy Warhol back in the early seventies. The classes consisted of weekly visits to the studios of these "blue chip artists" followed by a discussion with them about their work.

Seeing their magnificent homes and gargantuan studios in person was the first time I realized that visual artists could be successful enough to have medieval Tuscan libraries, reassembled brick by Florentine brick, in midtown lofts. A few weeks into the semester the good-looking TA mysteriously vanished, and Klaus made a joke about how the poor guy couldn't adjust to the fast pace of New York City. We all laughed, and when Klaus asked a student in the class to be his temporary assistant, the rest of us were stung with jealousy. Klaus began chatting with me during class breaks, mainly about contemporary art and painting. He found out I was a painting major as well, and I was supremely flattered when he asked me to email him photographs of my work.

One winter evening, on the last day of our class, Klaus asked me to stay back after the others had left.

"You have talent," he said, flicking through the images I had emailed him some weeks before. "A true gift."

"Thank you!"

"Oh, you're blushing," he said. "You know, I could use a gifted man like you with my next project. I'm not sure there is space, but for you . . . what are your plans after graduation?"

"None yet," I said, ignoring that sense of fatal anxiety that all graduating seniors who are not finance majors know so well.

"I'm working on major book project this year, commissioned by ze MoMA. Would you be interested to be my research assistant? Ze other one"—he gestured vaguely to his empty office—"didn't last very long. I'll even make sure your name on ze cover of ze book! What?" He grimaced when he saw my blank expression. "Not interested?"

"No!" I said. "I mean, yes! Of course I'm interested! It's just that . . ."

"Yes?"

"I'm not a US citizen," I confessed. "I only have a year after graduation to work here."

"Pfft!" he said, patting my back. "I'm sure we can extend that with ze right paperwork."

"Really?"

"Of course!" he said, as if visas were available at vending machines. "Done it dozens of time. Being me haz its perks. Und of course, it wouldn't just be ze research you'd be doing. I'd love to show your artwork to all ze major galleries in New York. By ze time we are done working together, Komail, you will be ze toast of ze town!"

Ayaan and Noor had both graduated from their respective colleges and moved into my Greenwich Village apartment some months earlier, and I rushed home to tell them the good news. Barely twenty-two, I'd landed a great job in my dream field! My name will appear on a book at the MoMA! Galleries and museums would flock to me! Success felt assured, as if fate herself was showing me the yellow brick road forward. I dismissed the fact that Klaus never discussed a salary or asked for any passport information as nothing more than self-sabotaging thoughts. *MoMA must deal with work visas*, I assured myself. *Banks do it all the time.*

Klaus wrote me a letter on his personal stationary announcing my participation in his project in case an immigration officers asked, but they never did. I began working for him immediately after returning from my coming out trip to Lahore. In those first few weeks he took me to many glittery New York art world events—museum galas, gallery openings, holiday parties at the homes of billionaire collectors— each, he insisted, integral to introducing me to the "right people." For what exactly, he never said, but in a world before social media allowed the comparative democratization of access, the art world ran on introductions from self-appointed but well-disguised gatekeepers. It still does, frankly.

It started with innocent looks, a glance held too long, a lingering touch as he handed over a file; I told myself I was imagining things, but after a month passed without salary or research, I began asking more pointed questions.

"Nothing to worry about," he assured me. "Slight delay the grant from ze museum, but when it come, then you won't have any time to rest! This is how it's done."

It must be, he knows everyone and everyone knows him, it must be.

"But if it's that much of a problem," he added in a low voice, "then please, you're *free* to take another job. I'll just have to write to ze immigration people, of course. No? Sure? Oh good."

Eventually he announced that we were to begin preliminary work out of his house in the Hamptons, which required me to trudge down every weekend to the snowy beach town from the city. He came to pick me up from the bus station accompanied by his previous assistant from class carrying her overnight bag.

"Aren't you staying?" I asked her.

"Nope," she said, flinging her luggage into the cargo hold of the bus. "Just the two of you." She was about to board when she paused and turned to me. "Be careful of him," she said quietly. "Klaus can be . . . tricky."

"Tricky?"

She was on the verge of saying more, but Klaus came up behind us and she boarded the bus without another word.

At twenty-two I was still the same weight as a juvenile whale but a full two feet taller. Having to cook my own food throughout college meant I ate far less of it, and for three glorious months in 2006 my cheekbones emerged too. Of course, it was never enough. After five years, a hundred pounds, and more pushups than should be legal, all it took was someone calling me "bitchtits" in the hallway for me to unravel into a spool of self-loathing. All of this to say that it never occurred to me that anyone would ever think of me as a trophy boy because, in my head, I looked like Imelda Marcos.

Klaus didn't think so. He slowly insinuated the topic of sex into our daily work conversation, casually mentioning ex-boyfriends before asking whether I was gay, that sort of thing. I said yes, hopeful that we could now talk as elder and student about queerness. He would violate the pedagogical dynamic purposefully, watching for a reaction whenever he said something deliberately racy. All I ever gave back was my resting bitchface. (A bit of a misnomer, really, since my bitchface never rests; my bitchface is ever vigilant.) One night in the Hamptons, I was changing into my pajamas when I saw a shadow shift under the slit of the guest bedroom door and I realized it was him trying to spy on me naked. I pasted a Band-Aid over the antique keyhole and turned off the lights. To confront him openly about it felt like too much of a risk, because what if I was mistaken and lost out on a great opportunity?

This went on for several weeks as I tried to figure out what to do about my increasingly dire predicament. Weeks of silent, sullen days and nights spent performing ignorance of his rancid intentions in an off-brand Hamptons home as I tried to salvage the burning wreckage of my career before it had even taken off. I feared it was already too late to apply for another job now, and besides, who would hire me with my visa issues? I didn't confide in anyone about what was happening with Klaus because I was too ashamed to have been tricked like this. *He wouldn't have done this to a straight boy*, I scolded myself in the chaos before sleep. *Never if you were straight*. It felt as if my gayness had betrayed me, offering me up as the naive boy prize to the kind of predatory hunters I saw on *Law and Order: SVU*. Except I wasn't a boy anymore; I was a strapping twenty-two-year-old man. How did this happen to me? How could I have been so blind?

Being broke can be a major inducement for professional clarity, and finally one day I told Klaus that if he wanted me to continue as his research assistant, I would have to start assisting on some actual bloody research and be paid for it. He relented and called me to his Manhattan apartment to pick up a suitcase of books. When I walked through his front door, he said hello and then, with the nonchalance of a smile, let his bathrobe fall down.

"I love you," he said, standing in the hallway stark naked.

I didn't immediately reply, distracted as I was by the foul mass of pink dough in front of me, and he mistook my silence as an opening.

"I think we'd make a great couple," he said, taking a step toward me. "Don't you see that I *love* you? I love your height, your brain, even your chest! Don't you see?"

"My . . . chest?"

The drive-by-shooting mention of my tits snapped me back to sordid reality. I realized then what I should have always known—that this geriatric walrus with alopecia had never intended for me to work for him at all. It all made sense now: the abrupt departure of his good-looking TA midterm, the practiced ease with which Klaus knew to wait until I was no longer technically enrolled at college to actively pursue me so as to avoid lawsuits, the constant references to my immigration status as hope and threat. This monster was trying to fuck me!

I threw the suitcase of books on the floor with a violence that surprised us both. He winced, looking both scared and aroused as I drew myself up to my full height and rearranged my features into an approximation of an angry Glenn Close. I wanted to destroy him, to demean him, to demolish every brick of dignity he had used to build this dome of lies.

All I managed to say was: "I quit."

The ring of his landline telephone pierced the tense silence that followed. He looked from the phone to me and back again. When he finally turned to answer it, I walked out of the apartment. The last time I saw him, Klaus was running naked down his building corridor, desperately trying to reach the elevator before the doors closed. Outside, in the busy purgatory of lunchtime in midtown Manhattan, I lit a cigarette. *You're a grown-up now*, I told myself as my hands trembled. *You'll be fine.*

Ayaan was on the futon watching Logo TV when I walked through the door of our apartment. "What happened?" he asked the moment he saw my face. I crumpled into a shivering mass on the floor and he held me in his arms as I bawled the truth. The next day I received an email from Klaus telling me he had written to US immigration services that I was no longer in his employ. I knew he hadn't done anything of the sort, of course—my student visa was not tied to his fictional job offer—but he didn't know that.

"You deserve to be deported back to that shithole you came from," was the last line of his email.

He's dead now.

The months I wasted on Klaus meant that Dependence Day was fast approaching. Like Ariel the mermaid, I too had to come to a new shore on a low budget and a time crunch to find a man to help me live far away from judgmental creatures in the dark deep. At least it worked out for her (more or less). I just couldn't figure out how people ended up getting the visas to live in America in perpetuity. When pressed, older acquaintances gave me unhelpfully vague responses, whispered nothings like "Merrill Lynch" or "Citibank" that were of no real use to my own situation.

"Where are you from, brother?" a taxi driver asked me one afternoon.

Shit.

Being called "brother" by another Muslim in a confined space makes me feel conspicuous and resentful. I generally avoided meeting

South Asians abroad in an effort to keep my Pakistani self discrete from my gay one (a lobotomy of shame that was probably also the reason I didn't have a boyfriend), but on that rainy spring day in a cab hurtling up Seventh Avenue I felt slightly homesick, and so I said, "Lahore."

"Me too!" he said with a grin, and launched into an uninterrupted monologue about his life. We went through his premature birth in a cow field, his trials at elementary school, and the beginning of his apprenticeship in a mechanic shop at age thirteen; we paused far too briefly to pontificate on how his stepmother poisoned his father with weed killer in order to clear the way for her to marry his uncle, after which we jumped to his first marriage to a cousin at sixteen and his second one to a neighbor's daughter at twenty. It wasn't until Forty-Ninth Street that his tale finally arrived in America.

"But how did you get to *stay* here?" I asked, now suddenly interested in this soap opera. His neck stiffened.

"You know," he mumbled airily. "Wife's family . . ."

"But didn't they die during the flood? Or was that your other wife? Was one of her relatives already a citizen? Did they sponsor you? How does that work exactly?"

It was obvious he was already regretting his decision to play jolly patriot on this ride, but we were both too deep in this now. He waited until the cab stopped at a traffic light before turning to face me in the back seat.

"Look," he said, his beady eyes darting around the crowded cross-streets. "I'm going to tell you a secret, but don't tell anyone, huh? *Sharam ki baath hai.*" It's a shameful thing.

He whispered so softly I had to press my head against the petri dish of plastic dividing us.

"Asylum."

"Asylum?"

"Shhhh!" he hissed, and locked the car doors to trap the word inside the cab's garlic-scented air with us. I felt immediately guilty for my knee-jerk dislike of him. For all I knew, this man had suffered through years of abuse at the hands of a motorcycle gang or a sanitation workers cult and had to flee to America in the middle of the night with nothing but his skin tags to live a life of peaceful dignity.

"I'm so sorry," I said with a hushed respect I usually only reserved for DMV workers. "That must have been difficult. There are *so* many people being persecuted back home just for who they are. I'm sorry you had to go through that."

"Wasn't that bad," he shrugged.

"Could I ask something? That is, only if you're comfortable telling me . . ."

"What?" he replied suspiciously.

"What kind of asylum did you apply for?"

"Oh," he said brightly. "I pretended to be a gay. Don't be so shocked," he added, catching my stunned expression in the rearview mirror. "Judge me if you want but it's a *great* way to get in. Some friends told me about it. Said that if you tell the Amreekans you're a *gandu*, they give you free visa to move!" He swerved to avoid a cyclist. "Sisterfucker! Think they own the whole goddamn street . . . where was I?"

"Gay asylum," I whispered.

"Oh *haan*! Asylum. *Yaar* must *hai*. I tried for years to get a visa but not a chance. Even lost all my savings when I trusted the wrong agency. They're all crooks at home, aren't they?"

"Quite."

"Are you all right?" he said, frowning at me. "You look sick. Don't be sick in the cab, huh? I'm not going through that again. *Acha*, so anyway, one day a man told us the embassy was giving visas to *gandus* to leave Pakistan and we thought, *chalo*, why not? So me and a friend pretended to be a couple—a few photos, some fake letters and *bus*, they gave us a visa. Just like that!" He snapped his fat fingers in the air.

"Aren't you . . . ashamed to use it like that?" I asked, swallowing my revulsion.

"It's not like we're really *gays*," he said, missing my point as deftly as he did the screaming pedestrians in front of us. "I mean, brother, you know, anything to leave Pakistan, right? Sure, we had to pretend to be like *khusras*, but in the long run—"

As instant as thought, I was back in that school parking lot, crowd of hecklers around me, Zariyan staring at the floor. The intervening years—the books, classes, the slow march to self-acceptance—gone like a drop of water in hot sand.

"They'll believe anything if you tell them what they want to hear," he finished, screeching to a halt at my destination. "Here we are, brother! What? Why no tip? Hey! HEY YOU! SISTERFUCKER!"

The conversation stayed with me for months. It poked at me on morning coffee runs, tortured me on long subway rides, whispered to me as I scoured job listings on Craigslist, and taunted me at gay bar happy hours. The opportunistic plasticity of the taxi drivers' homophobia was wrong but also, I knew from experience, commonplace. For him, like many other immigrants, the possibility of migration trumped various bigotries. If they had to pretend to be gay to get into the West, then so be it. If they had to pretend to accept women's rights, or religious plurality, or even blasphemy against their religion to leave Pakistan, many would do it willingly and without any sense of hypocrisy.

I had briefly thought about applying for asylum myself, but that route meant not returning to Pakistan for at least ten years, and I couldn't bring myself to make that stark a choice between my home and my self. Not then, at least. A college friend even offered to marry me for the passport, but I declined, not simply because I was convinced the INS would see through our application ("a gay fraternity, you say?") but because pretending to be straight to get the passport felt like a cowardly capitulation to the heteronormative oppression I was trying to escape in the first place. I'm not that idealistic anymore.

The incident with the taxi driver left me feeling irate enough to stop waiting for fictional magazine jobs, and I applied instead for a fellowship at a human rights organization in a department that focused on global LGBTQ+ rights. The work was rewarding and devastating: keeping discreet tabs on the whereabouts of fifty-two Egyptian men arrested and charged for the crime of being at a gay disco party on a boat; researching the circumstances around a gay Ugandan couple clobbered to death for living together; finding out that the Jamaican activist I had spoken with on my first day was found in pieces at the bottom of a well three months later; advocating for yet another trans woman jailed in the guaranteed violence of a male prison in New York for doing little more than standing on a street corner. The most painful part was reading the daily emails from queer folks all around the developing world pleading for a letter, an email, anything with an official logo that might help them get a visa to escape their individual hells. Their obvious desperation was a twin of my own, and also why I took my inability to help them as a personal failure.

I witnessed there firsthand the limits of human rights nonprofits, well-meaning places filled with well-meaning people where deserving cases often fell through the cracks of over-caution because of bureaucratic reticence, budget cuts, local politics, or the threat of bad optics. It was debilitating to see only tiny increments of slow change. I also learned there that an office job in a place as meaningful as a human rights organization was still just an office job, and so soul crushing did I find interacting with a photocopier that it was perhaps a mercy that my passport prohibited me from being eligible for most office work in America.

Ayaan moved back to Lahore to begin his journey to pop stardom (his talents at mimicry extended to his vocal range). Noor, meanwhile, was accepted to an MFA program in Brooklyn, and together we moved across the Manhattan bridge into a dank, cockroach infested apartment in pregentrified Williamsburg. He sported a scraggly beard now (a relic from his hippy friends at college) but looked otherwise unchanged. Every morning we walked together to the subway where I caught the train to work and he one to attend his classes. At night we'd reconvene for fat joints, greasy Chinese take-out food, and nature documentaries. On hungover weekends, we went to the Met to make drawings of the statues in the Greek and Roman wing.

Having a presence as familiar as Noor at such a precarious time in my life was comforting, but a decision still loomed. As the visa expiration ticked ever closer, I finally decided that if I was going to spend eight hours of my life sitting under unflattering lighting in binding waistlines, it might as well be under my own timings. Unwilling to return to Pakistan armed with nothing but an undergraduate degree and a sense of bitterness, I applied for a master's program in painting so I could attempt an art career in earnest. At the time the application felt like the next logical step in my future, and not the momentous decision to become a creative professional I now see it to be. The night I found out I'd been accepted into several art schools, one of them coincidentally at the same university Noor was attending, I cried on our fire escape, not just at the prospect of finally studying painting unfettered by distractions, but also out of relief that I would now be eligible for a fresh student visa. I had a reprieve. Maybe this time I'd be lucky, maybe this time I'd stay.

Art school is just as fun as you think it is. People dress fantastically (some even well), everyone doodles on their textbooks, and there is a pleasing sense of generalized anxiety coursing through a whole student body quite aware that graduating with an art degree means everyone is more or less equally fucked. The art school itself reminded me of a less aggressive version of the Academy, set as it was on a large, beautifully maintained campus. We were each assigned individual studios, bare rooms that would become the brief centers of our universe for the next two years.

I was making oil paintings using the vocabulary of Christian religious art to illustrate stories from Islamic lore to understand my own relationship with religion and the ways in which my identity directly affected my experience in America. I taught myself how to apply gold leaf, how to build altar pieces, how to apply glazes, and when not to light a cigarette near flammable materials. American art school curriculums have little technical instruction and are mostly premised on the concept of regular studio critiques, where a professor leads the class in a visit to your studio so people can air their opinion about any new work you've made that week. Fair warning: A lot of the art at art schools is utterly nauseating, and most of the crits quickly became an exercise in self-control.

"My work is about the complexity of human frailty interpreted through the second-wave feminist model of the birthing canal," someone would say, to which you might reasonably ask, as I did, "How exactly does a cucumber on a toilet seat do that?" But critiques are meant to be helpful, if not encouraging, and one is expected to say something constructive despite the rising nausea.

My memories from art school are some of the most precious I have, and I think of my time there fondly and often. But during my second semester I began to notice something strange: Whenever the class came to visit my studio, otherwise loquacious students would fall completely quiet. As much as I'd like to think that was because I was just so talented that the only natural reaction to my work was awed silence, that wasn't it. I reasoned that the silence may be because most of my paintings were about the burden of a Muslim identity under the gaze of American imperialism, and perhaps that *is* a bit in your face for nine A.M. But soon enough it was clear that the same wordlessness was happening in the studios of other people of color too. Eventually it became difficult to ignore the fact that while my white American colleagues spoke expansively about each other's pieces, dutifully identifying abstract expressionist influences or postmodern imagery with microscopic precision, they would invariably fall mute in front of work by non-white or non-American artists—the art that didn't center them directly. This is usually what happens when whiteness is made to feel its own otherness. Stripped of the familiarity of centrality, the students assumed that what they saw must be peripheral. Surely if the work was important enough then they would be in it. The underlying assumption here, and in the West in general, is that only work speaking directly to whiteness can ever be considered general discourse. Academics would later call this phenomenon the Silent Room. I just called it irritating.

It was difficult to articulate this to myself at the time because I knew I was privileged even in my exclusion. I was the only South Asian person in my class. Was it fair then for me to demand that my fellow students and teachers inhabit my world? Yes, I know now, it was. My experience was as valid as theirs, and their refusal to grapple with it had more to do with laziness than inability, like when a pretentious professor insisted on calling every student in class by their last names except me because mine was simply too long, despite their having managed to enunciate Dostoyevsky three times in ten minutes.

The less my colleagues spoke, the more confrontational my work became, so much so that by the end of art school I was painting historical scenes so intentionally steeped in obscure Islamic mythology that my thesis advisor said, "I don't know what to say in case I offend someone," which, I suppose, is a victory for art reflecting on the perils of blasphemy and loss of faith.

As I approached the end of art school, I gleaned that most gallery owners in New York didn't want to be shamed for not knowing who Imam Hussain was; they wanted to see you smear a sellable abstract line of thick paint and call it form. Figurative art was often considered an outdated genre when I was in art school, a relic of a history long since resolved. My pet theory is that this was because white folks truly believed that their own bodies were not political. Only the bodies of people of color are charged with carrying that particular burden, which is also perhaps why some of us gravitate toward representational art in the first place: to stand witness to what others cannot see.

After graduation, my art school friends all left New York City for painting residencies in the Appalachian Mountains or sculpture studios in New Mexico while I refreshed job postings with the enthusiasm of a bank teller. If you thought being a writer is a tough gig, you should try telling prospective employers you've majored in oil painting. The silence is symphonic. Exhausted by the continued burden of a Pakistani passport in a world where most years it ranked better only than a stack of Post-its, I flew back to Lahore to see my parents for three weeks in December 2010. We were out for a walk when we found out.

"*What?*" my father said loudly into the phone. "When? Are you sure? Oh God."

The governor of Punjab had just been murdered, shot seventeen times in his chest outside a small restaurant in Islamabad by one of his personal guards as the rest of his security force looked on impassively. The murderer was calmly arrested afterward and later told the press that he had killed the governor because of his recent support for the release of an impoverished Christian woman wrongly accused of blasphemy. A good Muslim, he claimed, shouldn't defend blasphemers.

To argue with the logic was to ignore how powerful radical elements in Pakistan had become since the American invasions. All over the country people were using the draconian blasphemy laws—introduced by the Dictator with Evil Eyebrows during his widespread Islamization of the country in the eighties—as an easy way to get rid of neighbors to take over their assets. To even be accused was tantamount to a death sentence, one often carried out by an irate mob well before the police pretended to intervene. The governor had been one of the first to publicly oppose this trend, and he paid for it with his life.

The death felt personal to me, as I know it did to many other Pakistanis, not simply because he was a well-known figure, but because his murder was a confirmation of how irreversibly the country's politics had shifted. In the awful days afterward, news anchors avoided using even the term "assassination" for fear of rousing the same mob that was now gathering in the hundreds of thousands to celebrate the murderer as a national hero.

By then I had been making paintings about blasphemy for years. Byzantine-inspired portraits of Muslim subjects against gold-leaf backgrounds that were my way of reconciling my fractured visual identity stretched painfully across two realities. What was the point, though? Brooklyn hipsters didn't care. America was bored of being made to feel bad about her treatment of Muslims and her foreign wars. Blasphemy for most Americans was a far-off threat in a far-off land. At the time most people chose to ignore the rumblings of

Hindutva hate in India, the parasitic populism in Europe, and the beginnings of MAGA and radicalization of the depressed white man in America. Obama had just been elected, the world was well, and everything was *fine*.

It didn't feel fine. I'm still not sure if it was an authentic response to the times or a mini stroke, but I decided that day that if I was to make work about the role of religion in my life, I should do it where it really matters.

Give me a sign, I asked the universe on my flight back to New York. *Any sign*. I returned to the apartment that I now shared with an Israeli friend to find that my room had been burgled through the fire escape, its contents thrown about like a Swedish art installation.

"Well," I said, sitting down on the spot where my computer used to be. "A bit heavy handed, but I get the hint. Back to Lahore."

As I packed eight years of my life into cardboard boxes, I couldn't shake the feeling of defeat. All that time in America and I still hadn't managed to carve out a permanent life for myself abroad, no more than I had been able to conjure a boyfriend. What would happen now? Was my being gay only something that existed when no one from Pakistan was looking? Was the only possible way to have a fully realized personal life to stay far away from Lahore forever, avoiding any confrontation with anyone who knew my parents so that I would spare them the pain of their disappointment and myself the agony of their rejection? If I did have a partner, would I subject our relationship to the same desecration?

I was fortunate to still have Jibran, Noor, and Ayaan, each of them as involved in the daily battles of my life as I was in theirs. But I knew other gay men from Pakistan, and one of the few shards of contention in my friendships with them was our diametrically opposed views on what it meant to be gay at all. Gay men in false marriages insisted that only they actually knew what was required to live in Pakistan, not privileged little brats like me. I was naive, they said, for thinking these allowances to tradition were compromises of cowardice, silly for constantly insisting that I didn't stop being gay just because I was on a different patch of land on earth, and willfully myopic for deliberately imposing "Western values" like an individual identity and personal freedom in a place that they so obviously didn't fit. After all, what examples were there? It was hard not to echo their belief that my very self was something that only existed in tenuously connection to the West Village and not, as I knew it to be, an inalienable right to my selfhood. For years I argued about this fundamental difference in perspective until I realized it's unfair to expect anyone else to understand your journey. It doesn't matter if they are acquaintances or family: You decide your path, and not everyone must follow you on it for it to make sense. Faced with my inevitable return to Pakistan, it was finally time to test that belief.

Noor, ever unbothered by mere trifles like existential self-doubt, surprised us all by being approved for an immediate green card based on his work as a painter and the prospect of a solo show in New York. That's how I found out a month before I was due to leave that artists can qualify for certain US immigration visas specifically designed to attract artistic talent. They were notoriously hard to get because the authorities needed hard evidence of fantastical career achievements. Noor's victory didn't surprise me, but I was not ready for the same because, apart from him and my parents liking my posts on Facebook, I had no actual career to speak of.

Still, I made an appointment with an immigration attorney before my flight back to Lahore, and she concisely walked me through the various options available for me to immigrate to the United States. After all the NSEERS interrogations during which I had to deny any such intent, it felt very strange to admit out loud the very basic fact that I wanted to live on in America. I walked out of the lawyer's office and into the bustling crowds of SoHo armed with the details of what I'd need for a visa based on talent, and the assurance that though I wasn't quite ready yet, there was no reason not to begin working on my application. When my case was sufficiently strong, I could always submit it from overseas. Yes, the lawyer assured me, even from Pakistan.

Speaking to her helped demystify a process I'd only ever envisaged in the haze of prayer. I sold one painting during my thesis show and used that money to set into motion an application that would become my lifeline for the next half decade. Taking those first concrete steps toward actual immigration (and what is a legal contract if not intellectual concrete?) helped assuage some of the anxiety I felt about leaving. Like Theseus walking into the Minotaur's labyrinth with a string attached to the exit, I too would have a tangible connection back to New York.

The lawyer cautioned me against haste. I should take my time, she said, make the best application I possibly could. If my petition was rejected for any reason, it would be years before I could apply again. Getting the green card this way may be a long shot, I knew, but it was also my only shot.

And so, nearly a decade after first leaving, I moved back into my childhood bedroom in Lahore, the *Buffy* poster still taped above my bed.

Chapter 11

A FAST BY THE FURIOUS

BY 2012, MOST OF THE fossilized hairdos on the local news described Pakistan as a democracy again. The media channels that the last military dictator had allowed to flourish under his reign had, in my absence, grown thorns enough to defend themselves. The military regime's tenure unraveled shortly after the tragic assassination of Benazir Bhutto (the country's first female prime minister and second gay icon), and her husband rode into the presidency on a wave of national sympathy over the shared loss of a fallen warrior, and the armed forces, who usually like to control such matters, let him.

Religious extremism had metastasized all around Pakistan's body politic. The weak civilian government was terrified of the near-military-grade power of the religious groups and kept handing them small concessions in the hopes that by allowing space, they'd be given some too. But bullies don't work that way, and those early years felt like a very abusive marriage where the threat of violence loomed constantly. The theatre of security went baroque as vast chunks of Pakistan's northern territories were overrun with Taliban militants and their supporters, the kind of men that shot Malala in the head for going to school, while Lahore—historically sheltered from major violence by a combination of rivers, denial, and feudal exceptionalism—suddenly found herself besieged by suicide bombers sent to terrorize Pakistan's urban centers as retaliation against its army's participation in America's war next door in Afghanistan. Most folks in the city ignored the specter of violence while going about their daily schedule, distracted as they were by soaring inflation and sixteen-hour blackouts, the unfortunate consequence of when army generals are left in charge of utilities for decades.

Congruently, many ordinary Pakistanis, forced to witness the witless decline of a country sucked dry by powerfully corrupt elites, found succor in remembering Islam's medieval-era dominion over the world. Shortly after I returned, the religious fringe forced the federal government to ban access to sites like YouTube, ostensibly to protest blasphemous content, but the real goal was to limit access to places on the internet not entirely ruled by their ideologies. Not that they needed an excuse; the Taliban sympathizers used any opportunity to flex their muscles. We rule this land, we heard them say with every new win for censorship.

Pakistan's overzealous commitment to that censorship was no better exemplified than when the Pakistan Telecommunication Authority (the national censorship board) released a list of phrases that they insisted could no longer be used on air or in print. Turns out you really don't know how much you wanted to say "crotch monkey" until you can't. I'll limit myself to the English words here, since the Urdu phrases were masterpieces unto themselves, the most glorious of which was the now sadly forbidden "sweat from the pubic hair of a lizard."

In addition to banning anything remotely related to sex (such a flexible word, bless it), the PTA also outlawed the terms "premature," "stroke," "yellow man," "kumquat," "uterus," "breasts," all variant spellings of the word "masturbate" except the correct one, "excrement," "lactate," "Kmart," "lap dance," "lolita," "man hater,"

"Jack the Ripper," "rear end," "Satan," "showtime," "slant," "snot," "spit," and, my personal favorite, "Purina Princess."

It was not lost on many that while the country was busy deciding who gets to say "syphilis" on air, no one could yet explain how Osama bin Laden—the worlds most wanted terrorist—had been caught living in an army compound well within Pakistan's borders. Though to be fair, they still haven't.

Absurdities aside, there were aspects of my return that I did relish, like the return to the Muslim shower, my favorite thing in the whole wide world. Essentially a small handheld water pump that you use to wash your privates, it is what I miss the most outside Pakistan, and sensing its cleansing, benevolent presence next to me on the loo is one of the surest signs I feel at Home. (I've long wondered how people who invented television could still consider wiping themselves with dry tissue paper to be in any way hygienic. It's deplorable. Do better.)

There were other advantages to being back in Lahore: the ticking clock of my US visa expiration had been replaced with a comfortably numb timelessness. There was no urgency to wake up in the morning because there was nowhere to go, no one made me feel guilty for eating fried food in between meals, and there was usually a *Grey's Anatomy* marathon on one of the Polish satellite television channels, assuming we had electricity that day.

My positivity lasted three days. Day four I went to a dance recital at an open-air stadium in Lahore, a rare cultural event that was free and open to the public. There was a traffic jam of armed guards outside the venue. "You aren't anyone in Lahore anymore unless someone is trying to kill you," I heard someone say as we walked past a small army of private security. Like most public audiences in the Islamic Republic, the crowd was all male. A smattering were probably older than twenty but nearly everyone else was still being pummeled by puberty. They stood in large packs eyeing each other like life was the opening act of *West Side Story*, and the steady buzz of conversation grew louder as more of the audience took their seats. When the curtains opened suspiciously on time, I thought to myself, *Isn't this nice? We're such a lovely people devoted to art and culture and all we need is to get out more!*

The lights went down (hooting, catcalls, one fart sound) as a woman stepped out onstage (show paused for ten minutes of louder hooting, sexist jokes, numerous fart sounds). After a short introduction that was quickly drowned out by an onslaught of pubescent screaming, the spotlights blazed on. A male dancer walked out onto the stage to noise that was not applause and assumed his stance to begin a performance of *kathak*, a traditional dance performed with anklets fitted with bells.

The chant was soft, easily mistaken for conversation at first, but as he danced it grew louder and louder. Eventually the tinkle of bells and the string of the sitar were drowned out by the audience hissing one word in unison: "*Khusra . . . Khusra . . . Khusra . . .*"

The dancer kept moving, his graceful limbs swaying beautifully, effeminately, and methodically.

"*Khusra! Khusra! Khusra!*"

I cringed for us both. Pakistanis are often mistrustful of public dance performances. Any non-wedding-related dancing is most often associated with prostitution, and local dancers are by extension viewed with puritan suspicion (to arrange a "private dance" is still code for paid sex). Eventually, the heckling got so loud that the organizers halted the show.

I didn't want to stay another moment, and when I got up to flee, I caught a glimpse of the dancer weeping offstage, his head hung low to a chorus of boos. I wanted to hug him tight, to whisper in his ear that he wasn't alone here. But a dance troupe from the Netherlands was waiting in the wings for their turn, and they emerged to thunderous, rapturous applause, because nothing shuts desi boys up like a white guy doing the moonwalk.

As the months dragged on and the weed wore off, the true reality of moving back to Lahore set in. I was confronted daily with such realities of living in the developing world as procuring driving licenses, opening a bank account, and paying bribes for parking tickets, each of which required a classical hero's journey of loss, heartache, and heatstroke. Nothing gets done in Pakistan's bureaucracies without a bored underling being given a presidential-level order, printed in triplicate, and signed in an ink made from the tears of a blood moon fairy caught at midnight. This slow pace of life is endemic to countries with hot climates (except Canada, which somehow has both arctic windchill *and* long lines) and eventually I accepted it with the same bitter resignation as I did the electricity cuts, rampant corruption, and the fact that to masturbate took at least an hour because it was someone's job in the Pakistani government to ban all porn sites ("Finally an office job one can enjoy!").

I took a part-time job writing a weekly column for a local English-language newspaper. The position paid nothing, but gave me a place to expel my growing bile. The editor had initially asked for the lighthearted perspective of someone just moving back, and I agreed on the conditions that (a) I choose my own topics, and (b) I use a pseudonym to protect myself from religious zealots and my mother's more litigious girlfriends.

Finding topics proved to be a bit of a challenge, particularly since I avoided going out anywhere in Lahore I might run into people I knew, partly out of laziness and partly to avoid the internalized shame I felt at having returned from America without possessing something impressive to show for my time there, like a Pulitzer

Prize or Ronan Farrow. In that sense, moving back to Lahore felt like being trapped inside a high school reunion that never ended. To fight against the behemoth of local culture by complaining of its shortcomings was to willfully ignore the reality of the resources around me, but even that naive pragmatism was tested during my first Ramadan.

For one month every lunar year, Muslims around the world observe Ramadan, the holy month of dieting, when everyone decides en masse to stop giving a single, solitary shit. They claim fasting is a voluntary act, but when enough people glare at you murderously whenever you so much as look at a bottle of Evian, it can all feel rather pointed. The whole Muslim world reorders itself during Ramadan: Alcoholics stop drinking, smokers stop smoking, adulterers stop adulting, even Grindr profiles evaporate into a pious puff of purity as people give up their homosexuality for the month like an addiction to dairy, all eyes now fixed on the minute hand of the clock as it edges closer and closer to sunset and the end of the fast. In the darkness of night, though, all bets are off.

I used to fast enthusiastically as a child as a way to control my expanding waistline as well as to experience a sense of belonging. You'd think that a month spent not eating or drinking during daylight hours in subtropical heat might have helped me lose a few pounds, but fasting only made me efficient at consuming more food in less time, like an elite speed eater. I have tremendous respect, even affection, for people who genuinely treat Ramadan as a spiritual detox. I am not one of those people.

3:45 A.M.: Alarm. Hit snooze.

3:47 A.M.: Alarm again.

3:49 A.M.: Dad enters bedroom, shakes me softly, and leaves.

3:57 A.M.: Mother barges in like invading US tank, switches off AC, and leaves door open to radiating heat in blatant act of unprovoked warfare.

4:01 A.M.: At dining table. Surly. No time to brush teeth. Family in suspiciously jovial mood given it is predawn, but prospect of food works like Prozac. Everyone is feasting on hodgepodge of toast, eggs, lamb curry, pulao, kebabs, and fruit, but I feel sick at mere thought of lamb curry before dawn so pick at an apple feeling Gwyneth-thin.

4:04 A.M.: Announce I'm not eating anything and on way back to bed congratulate self on righteous decision in face of rampant poverty and unequal economic distribution of wealth in world.

4:11 A.M.: Guzzle entire bottle of water in preparation for coma. Nothing better than when you can sleep again after being unduly woken up. Ah. Holy Month.

4:16: A.M.: Dawn *azaan* begins from loudspeakers of nearby mosque. Feels like am in the opening credits of *Lawrence of Arabia*. Very much ethnic splendor and diversity.

4:18 A.M.: Hm. Getting a bit loud now. Also is completely not synchronized with two other *azaans*.

4:19 A.M.: I mean really, how many mosques are there within a mile?

4:26 A.M.: For fuck's sake. There are *fourteen* different *azaans* going simultaneously and whole off-key production now sounds like indecipherable Bjork performance. Try to suffocate self with pillow.

4:33 A.M.: *Azaan(s)* have stopped, thank God for silence.

4:37 A.M.: Was trap. Mosque closest to house now doing *azaan* techno remix.

4:43 A.M.: Techno remix replaced by wailing medical siren to announce official beginning of fast.

4:49 A.M.: Silence?

4:50 A.M.: OK. Yeah. Sleep. Finally!

5:01 A.M.: Ugh. Have to pee now.

5:10 A.M.: Could totally eat the lamb curry, to be honest.

5:14 A.M.: Telling myself the pain of hunger I'm feeling is simply tingle of belly burning fat. Is this what thin feels like?

5:32 A.M.: I mean, one really should be able to have a sip of water at least. Sun isn't even totally visible in the sky yet.

9 A.M.: Alarm! OMG, what? Who died?

9:01 A.M.: Mouth feels dry and cakey, like petri dish of unfulfilled desires. God, I'm so thirsty.

9:13 A.M.: Spend ten minutes brushing teeth in hopes that I can trick mind into thinking am hydrated.

9:14 A.M.: Power just went out again. Feel Bolshevik anger at cruel government that would enforce the tyranny of hourly electricity cuts in midsummer on whole country already in throes of caffeine withdrawal.

9:15 A.M.: Does swallowing toothpaste make the whole fast void? Google says yes, but also corporations lie. Better to be minty.

9:25 A.M.: In car headed to air-conditioned newspaper offices. Decided to skip going to art studio today as still have no AC there and cannot fathom sitting in pool of my own sweat until sundown. Have nothing to actually do at office since have no desk, but they once offered use of their industrial printer, and it gives me somewhere to go other than sofa. Skipping breakfast actually saves a lot of time in the morning. Who knew?

9:42 A.M.: God, I'm so thirsty.

9:47 A.M.: Wish they would let me write column on how difficult it is to buy condoms in Lahore. Last pharmacy I tried demanded a marriage certificate and then tried to sell me party balloons instead.

9:55 A.M.: Stuck in traffic. Commuters on a fast are not happy people.

10:15 A.M.: Arrived at office but editor slightly bewildered by my presence as I am not technically an employee (#gatekeepers) but pointed me toward a spare desk in corner anyway.

1:10 P.M.: Spent last hours trying to watch *Dreamgirls* performances online but woman at next desk gave me angry lecture about office bandwidth. Internet says fast won't end until 7:26 P.M. today, which feels decades away.

1:14 P.M.: I'll be fine! Fast is nearly half done, after all. I'll be fine.

1:16 P.M.: I'm not fine.

1:22 P.M.: Desk neighbor is still giving me sideways glances of judgment.

1:35 P.M.: OMG, just caught her sneaking sips of mineral water under her desk when she thought no one was looking!

1:36 P.M.: Bitch.

1:37 P.M.: Remind myself that fasting is a choice, religion is personal, and it's none of my business if she is keeping the *roza* or not. Am complete within myself, especially since doing this more as nationally enforced agnostic diet than fulfillment of Abrahamic tradition. Isn't it shocking, though, how quickly righteous anger can take root? Maybe this is why religious policing feels like opiate, since it gives you ever more reasons to hate someone who is not you.

1:47 P.M.: It's lunch hour somewhere out there in the eating world. Imagine myself like actress from *American Beauty*, lying on floor as shower of Pringles crisps cascade across my naked, strategically covered body.

2:15 P.M.: Just spent last half hour on YouTube (praise VPNs) learning how potato chips are made, which led me to video on how to make gourmet crisps at home, which led me to Nigella Lawson baking honey-glazed chicken.

2:16 P.M.: Desk neighbor just gave me another lecture on bandwidth. As if her article on ongoing constitutional crisis is *that* bloody urgent.

2:18 P.M.: Look at Nigella pour that honey, though.

2:19 P.M.: I want honey. I want honey so bad I could eat it off someone. I want to lick honey off a gorgeous man's body, just throw a hunk into a vat and watch the liquid gold as it drips over his perky pecs and down the ripples of his taut stomach till it touches the veiny tip of his glistening, hard, throbbing . . . OK, wow . . . that is not a pious thought. Is one meant to police one's mind as well as one's appetite during a fast? Surely not. Is that what believers actually do during Ramadan? Get up at dawn and spend the rest of the day trying not to think about sex and food?

2:20 P.M.: Probably.

2:21 P.M.: Ew, though.

2:22 P.M.: But then, why *am* I doing this? After all the years I spent snorting with derision at the Muslim Students Associations extolling the virtues of fasting at college fairs, why am I now keeping up with the practice of a religion I do not practice? What's stopping me from just eating burgers and jerking off in bed all day like I want to do? A sense of duty? To whom? My mother? This country? No, nothing as pedantic as that, I hope. Remind myself that today is about self-discipline and belonging. The discipline to remind myself that if I don't belong it's not because I'm incapable of it, but because I choose not to. Then the rejection works both ways.

2:23 P.M.: On second thought, maybe it *is* about my mother . . .

2:35 P.M.: Thought spiral interrupted as video stalls again because VPN slows the internet down. Oh how I wish they stopped banning websites. Is useless strategy, like building a large, expensive gate in an open field.

3:05 P.M.: Feeling so sleepy. Let me just rest head down on the desk for a quick moment.

4:35 P.M.: What happened? Who am I? Who died?!

4:36 P.M.: Water neighbor roughly nudged me awake to say office is closing and I have to leave. Sense heat of anger the full-time workers are sending my way for doing little more than using printer once every three months but no longer care. At least they all get paychecks.

Leaving today feeling like a productive albeit decaffeinated member of society.

4:45 P.M.: In cab headed home now.

4:58 P.M.: No air-conditioning in car. Seat covers smell like rotting onions.

5:03 P.M.: I think I may die in this Suzuki.

5:05 P.M.: So thirsty . . .

5:14 P.M.: Ahhh. Home!

5:16 P.M.: Now what?

5:24 P.M.: No one in family talking to each other so decide to avoid conflict and watch cooking show marathon, which during a fast feels like tantric eating.

6:59 P.M.: Oh God, am so hungry and angry and anxious and sad and bloated and fat and horny. Everything is awful and everyone hates me. *Khala* Boob was right, am never going to find love and will only ever live a C+ life.

7:15 P.M.: Can sense *iftari* is close since house is buzzing. Help everyone bring dishes to the table like *My Big Fat Greek Wedding*. Love *iftari*, when the fast ends, as is only true meal where one can eat endlessly without any judgment whatsoever. Lots of favorites on the table: crispy *pakoras*, flaky samosas, breaded potato cutlets, fried chicken tenders, *namak paras*, onion rings, biryani, *aloo gosht*.

7:25 P.M.: Whole family is seated now, staring at steaming food with vacant expressions. Am twirling a chicken tender under my nose like a smoker flirting with a vape pen.

7:26 P.M.: No sign of *azaan*.

7:27 P.M.: Still no sign of *azaan*.

7:28 P.M.: Where the fuck is *azaan* when you actually need it?

7:31 P.M.: Feel jilted by internet! I swear I'm going to cut off . . . oh yay! Just heard call to prayer! Feel like champion winner of a religious marathon! Am going to ignore the tradition that Shias break their fast ten minutes later as surely is the thought that counts . . .

7:58 P.M.: OMG. Inhaled whole table.

8:01 P.M.: Internet says there are seventy calories in one *pakora*. I ate fourteen before I even started on the appetizers. Oh god! Oh god! Oh god!

8:03 P.M.: Think of general calories I didn't eat throughout day though! It *must* even out in end, right?

8:04 P.M.: Right . . . ?

8:05 P.M.: Mother just came out with the most enormous cheesecake I've ever seen.

8:06 P.M.: I mean, one slice won't kill me. It's been such long day.

8:25 P.M.: Am fat monster who will never ever find love. Hate that to find relationship as gay man is toxically related to having single digit body fat percentage. NOT ALL OF US LIKE CARDIO, SEAN CODY! That's it. I'm never going to watch food programs again.

9:36 P.M.: Feeling a bit peckish, honestly.

9:49 P.M.: Mmm, cheesecake really was so good. So sleepy . . .

3:45 A.M.: Alarm. OMG WHAT HAPPENED?

3:55 A.M.: No. There is no way I'm keeping another fast. Fuck off.

Most people only make it through Ramadan by looking forward to Eid, the holiday that marks the end of the month of restraint with three days of unbridled gluttony. (There actually two Eids a year: the one at the end of Ramadan is the Small Eid, while the Big Eid takes place two months later, after the Hajj, and requires a serial killer's affection for red meat.) Eid remains one of the only occasions Pakistanis are officially encouraged to celebrate, in no small part because it aligns with the country's religious branding. Eid traditionally begins, for men at least, with an early morning Eid prayer, but mandatory masculine forays into misty mosques on the wrong side of six A.M. were never my best look, and I've suffered through enough early morning communions to know that I'm not a strong enough person to pray so close to so many people farting in synchronicity, and so I don't.

The only thing to do after Eid prayers is to eat, sleep, and prepare for the Visitations. Eids are the only times of the year, other than the occasional death, when the dark-intentioned and usually dispersed ghosts of my extended family float across in portentous unison to haunt my parents' house with cakes, cards, and carefully constructed insults. Painful as the visits were ("Still not married? Why don't you play more sports? You mean you paint houses?"), I looked forward to them in the way I imagine computers do a mandatory software update. How else would I know that Cousin Ahmed is now rumored to be in jail in Croatia for defrauding a nightclub? Or that Uncle Mushtaq's son was expelled from school for violating a pumpkin? Or that Aunty Pepsi has been having wine for breakfast since 1974? (Because I know you're going to ask: *khala* Boob's sister, *khala* Cherry, nicknamed her own firstborn girl Pepsi because, and I quote, "her skin was as dark as a bottle of cola"—a revelation that is shocking on many levels, not least because it proves *khala* Boob was not the nastiest person in the family.)

But some Eid visits were more informative than others.

"Is that Komail I see hiding back there?" a woman's voice asked from somewhere inside a group of visitors that had just invaded our home armed with a tres leches cake. I recognized the voice immediately, frightening and familiar as any childhood trauma: Tara, my bowl-cut nemesis, she of the Barbies, tantrums, and *The Little Mermaid* viewings. "Oh my Gawd," Tara shrieked as if we'd run into each other in outer space purely by chance. "It *is* you!" After everyone air-kissed, both our sets of parents ambled into the lounge, leaving Tara and me alone. A gentle breeze came out of nowhere to blow the tresses of her shiny long hair as she walked toward me in slow motion, her tiny but flawless face already in full contoured makeup by noon. Her long fake eyelashes accentuated her light-gray contact lenses, ones that she had no doubt color matched precisely with the tight gray *kameez* now hugging the curves of her toned body like a bitter grudge.

"Hello, Tara." I nodded, dripping with resentment. "You look nice."

"Oh, please!" she said, fluttering her lashes like a bitchy Bambi. "Haven't even had time to wash my face this morning. But look at *you*!" She stood back, scanned me up and down, and changed the subject. "You know, when Mother told me you'd moved back to Lahore, I told her, 'No way would Komail come back!' Not with all the **cruel pause** . . . *fun* I hear he's been having in New York!'" The sound of laughter came from the next room. "So," she asked, walking arm in arm with me like two Victorian ladies taking a turn about the room, "couldn't hack it in the States after all, huh?"

We stared at each other.

"It's difficult to stay on in America these days," I said.

"So I hear," she said with a painfully fake expression of sympathy. "*We* all have US passports, but the irony is I hardly ever go!" She roared with visa-free delight. "But anyway, what on *earth* are you doing these days? Tell me, tell me! Do you *still* like dressing up in girls' clothes?"

First blood.

"I'm writing for a newspaper," I said, ignoring the bait. "But mostly I'm working on my next show at the gallery." For all she knew, "the gallery" could mean MoMa and not, as was the truth, the top floor of a sofa shop.

"Amazing," Tara said with disinterest. "So *brave* for you to become an artist. All that uncertainty. Never knowing when you'll eat next or if—"

"I don't think—"

"—you'll ever make any money. I'm quite traditional that way. Need my three meals and nice things."

"I do actually—"

"But then again you always *were* different, weren't you? Remember? Remember how you used to play with my dolls all the time? Do you remember the dolls?"

"Yes," I muttered, reflexively looking around to make sure no one had overheard her. "Yes, I remember."

"So," Tara said. "Do you have a *girlfriend* in Lahore yet?"

It was an innocuous question, I suppose. Had I been asked it by a stranger at a party, I probably wouldn't have felt the same shame color my cheeks. But I knew how Tara hunted. The years had honed her childhood cruelty into a more evolved weapon, like a long-forgotten prehistoric but passive-aggressive shark still hunting the oceans for that one blowfish it used to torture in infancy (love blowfish, wish I could go from beachball to a size two with an exhale). I took a deep breath and reminded myself that I was out now. My sexuality wasn't a shame, her bigotry was.

"No," I replied. "You?"

"Funny," she said without smiling. "No, I'm married now, actually. Didn't you know?" She held up her left hand to show off a giant sapphire trapped in a circle of obese diamonds.

"Congratulations," I said.

"His name is Bilal," she went on. "Bilal Sadiq. He went to the Academy too, though as I remember you didn't have many friends there, so you may not have known him."

She is such a little . . . but wait. Wait! A realization dressed in sequins and slathered in glamor slid into my mind on a rainbow of happiness, a deduction so glowing and perfect that I completely forgot to be offended at her latest insult.

"Bilal, you said?" I asked, barely repressing a grin. "Bilal Sadiq?"

"Yes," she replied, beaming smugly.

"Bilal *Ahmed* Sadiq," I pressed on. "About this tall, played basketball in high school, lived in the house behind the park on F road with the U-shaped garden at the back?"

"Y-yes," she said again, her smile beginning to waver. "So you *do* know him?"

Oh, this was too good. This was too *easy*!

"Oh, I *know* him," I said, now positively bursting with joy.

"You do?"

"I do," I said, leaning in uncomfortably close to her fake lashes. "I really, *really* do."

"How?" she said, her guard now completely down.

I imagined the devastated look on Tara's face when I revealed to this fistula that her precious husband Bully Bilal was as gay as an Italian jockstrap, the crushed expression I would relish in revenge for all the torture both of those monsters had inflicted on me. I imagined her confronting him later that night with my revelation of his past, and what lies Bully Bilal would concoct to conceal his truth, the tales he would spin to explain their no-doubt-vacant sex life, the explanations he would invent for the long absences from home that she would now dissect with retroactive suspicion, the vacant excuses he would give for having downloaded Grindr on his phone, the debris of her puerile social aspirations that would now fall around her just like the barbed arrows she'd spent a lifetime shooting out from her high tower of judgment. Oh, how *just* life can be! How truly fair!

Just then a young maid who had been sitting in an adjoining room came up to us carrying a crying baby in her arms. "Ma'am," she said to Tara, swinging the newborn from side to side. "I think baby wants to see you."

"Not now," said Tara, ignoring the woman.

"But ma'am—"

"Take him away," she hissed, and turned back to me. "Komail, how do you know my husband? Exactly?"

She already knew. Deep down, beneath the years of casual cruelty, callous calm, and caramel contour, Tara already knew that her husband was gay. Her life was a capitulation to the cult of conformity into which both she and Bully Bilal had been indoctrinated in since birth. And though it might make me feel momentarily better to walk through the burning embers of her smoldering dreams, I also knew that was not my job. Her facade would crumble in time, but its destruction would not be my burden.

"Everybody knew him," I said, backing down. "He was very popular."

She was on the verge of asking me something more, but the need for conformity reaffirmed its grip on her, and she regained her menacing stare, temporarily reassured of her perch high above all others.

"Tara!" Her mother called from the next room. "Come here and show Aunty and Uncle the pictures from your trip to Sitges with Bilal!"

Chapter 12

GOOD MOURNING

*L*IVING IN THE SAME HOUSE as my family confirmed rather quickly that to avoid being the sole survivor of a messy but cathartic massacre, I would need to move out.

But I didn't have enough money to live on my own, so I lay awake every night in looping anxiety spirals trying to figure out a way to monetize my art degree. After some abortive attempts at finding studio space in Lahore ("What do you mean a family of ten lives in the back?"), I found an unoccupied house halfway across town. My parents dubbed the place Bridgebottom, given that it was situated, quite literally, directly beneath a soaring highway bridge. No one had lived there for years, which meant that there were no working outlets, gas, or running water, but it was an escape.

After several months spent smoking up and then crying into my turpentine-soaked rags, I was eventually offered a show at a local gallery. It wasn't particularly well received, but it led some months later to another show, and that to another. Very slowly, I was able to scrape together a modest living doing the one thing I'd always been told would never bring in any money.

Living on your own is an exceptionally unusual thing to do in Pakistan, a place where I've seen sixty-year-olds throw violent temper tantrums because their mothers hadn't cooked their favorite dish right. Setting up a home from scratch requires more resources than is fair, but fortunately, my gold-leaf paintings that used beautiful men to explore homosexuality under the guise of religious art were selling well. By my fourth gallery show, I had saved enough money to embark on the Herculean process of renovating Bridgebottom into a place I could live full-time.

There is a scene in *The Princess Bride* where Carey Elwes and his fabulous hair are taken to a subterranean dungeon and strapped into a machine that sucks literal time away from the victims' lifespan in painful, permanent bursts. Renovating a home is like being strapped into that machine, and the process drains away far more from your soul than mere money. Renovating a closet costs a month of your life. Want to redo the bathrooms? Two years. A whole floor? Death is quicker.

I spent my first night at Bridgebottom on a mattress with a tooth-brush and two forks. A friend recommended a contractor named Salamat to help me in the renovations, a pencil-thin man with four tobacco-stained teeth who was a wizard at everything from build-ing bookshelves to kitchens. At the beginning of our joint venture, Salamat and I spent long, happy hours going over color theory and a mood board of Aegean blues as we spoke about the Look of the Loo or my vision for a lounge that was both rococo *and* midcentury. During all our long and, in retrospect, fairly one-sided conversations, Salamat nodded and smiled, leaving me with the strong but misguided impression that we were aesthetic twins separated at birth, and it was only after he tiled my entire bathroom with a printed pattern that looked like a marching band of pink vaginas that I discovered that this might not be the case.

But we kept working together; he was quick, up-front, and, above all, wickedly funny. Over the next two years, Salamat and I went through the house room by room—laying new floors, polishing cabinets, replacing the kitchen sink, installing working toilets, really anything I could afford to do at the time—until Bridgebottom slowly went from looking like an underachieving serial killer's basement to a quasi-cozy domicile.

The news that a young single man was living by himself in the dilapidated house at the end of the road was met with euphoric suspicion by my new neighbors, a gaggle of widowed grandmothers who went on daily evening walks in a tight geometric formation. They looked so much like a geriatric sixties girl group that I called them the Abracadavers.

We first met when they barged through my front door like a gust of jealousy, leaving me mouthing the words "personal space" soundlessly as they fanned out through the rest of the house with the speed of bounding ninjas. *What are you doing here? How much was this door? Are you married? How much is the electric bill for this place? Is this double bed only for you? Why don't you have a dining table? Not even one wife? How much was that microwave? Oh . . . big spender! Children these days don't know the value of money. When I was your age we used to eat glass. When will you get married? What's your family's history? What did your grandfather do? Was he married? What do you mean "twice"?*

It was only when I asked them to watch their ankles because my pet snake was missing that the Abracadavers begrudgingly tiptoed out the door. In what a real estate agent would later describe as an "adjoining economic opportunity," Bridgebottom also had the misfortune of standing at the base of a ludicrously large billboard that was perpetually rented to KFC. And though I personally loved waking up to the sight of a sizzling fried chicken thigh every morning, the visuals wreaked absolute havoc on my dietary willpower. But none of that mattered, because Bridgebottom was a sanctuary of my own, and for the first time since my return, I felt I could breathe again. Not too deeply, of course, because highway fumes are a real concern.

Many who live in climates like Pakistan's do so with some form of help—the dust alone would keep one cleaning all day—and as in all things, Salamat came to my rescue when he conjured a distant cousin from his village who needed work in the city. And so it was that a one-eyed diabetic named Tariq, illiterate but whip-smart, moved in to help me run the house in exchange for a steady salary and room and board. I'd long been opposed to live-in help for fear of being outed. Living alone was no real guarantee of safety as a gay man, and I knew that all Tariq had to do was whisper the wrong things at the right mosque for a mob to materialize outside my home demanding a trial by fire. The same thing was happening all over the country to religious minorities; was it so much of a stretch to think it could happen to me?

But Tariq was professional and pleasant and prepared a spectacular lamb curry. And while his benign presence allowed me more time to work, it did threaten to curtail my blossoming sex life. The big upshot of living alone was that I now had a safe place to hook up with guys in privacy. And so hook up I did. A lot.

Grindr's popularity was still nascent when I left New York, but it had already changed the way gay men connected all around the world. Most millennials—broke, horny, and on a steady cocktail of antianxiety medication—welcomed a change from the tribal ritual of eye-fucking that had dominated queer courtships in the scantily dressed nineties. With hookup apps you could easily chat with people nearby from the safety of your bathroom, sharing only the best-lit, best-edited version of yourself before meeting. But Grindr was so much more than just a proximal hookup app. In places where cruising the wrong person in public is potentially lethal (I'm looking at you, Wyoming), Grindr offered a digital Zion unfettered by the strictly enforced divisions of class, caste, and even language that rigidly order socialization in so much of the straight world.

My first good liaison was with a beverage waiter at a catering company who began chatting with me on his way out from a late-night wedding. We traded the necessary pics and coordinated his arrival for after I was sure Tariq had gone to bed. He arrived on time, a dark hulking beauty of man, and I led him wordlessly into my bedroom, where we pounced on each other's naked bodies. After several rounds of sex so feral even I forgot to be self-conscious about my body, we lay intertwined in my bed sharing a cigarette as he spoke about his job, his goals, his engagement. He'd recently moved to Lahore from a small town several hours away to work as a clerk in a bank, but when that didn't pan out his friend got him the catering job.

"It's good business," he said. "Lots of rich people throw events here all the time. The drunker they get the more they tip."

"How long do you want to stay in Lahore?"

"At least until I get married," he said, carefully extinguishing a half-smoked cigarette and saving it in a folded tissue paper.

"Does your fiancé know?"

"Know what?" He looked genuinely curious.

"About . . . well," I gestured at our naked bodies.

He grinned. "What's *that* got to do with anything?"

"Nothing, I suppose."

I felt him watching me as I leaned over to light another cigarette. "Are you married?" he asked.

I shook my head, blowing out the smoke toward the ceiling in a sharp gray cone. "No."

"Oh," he said. "I just assumed because of the house . . ."

"Why the house?"

"Unmarried men live with their parents," he said. It wasn't a question.

"I'm new here," I lied.

"Ohhhhh," he said, eyes widening in comprehension. It still surprised me how immediately explicable I became to other Pakistanis once they believed I was some kind of foreigner. Admitting my unbelonging to them allowed any confusion over my motives or history to resolve itself in their minds with satisfying neatness. I, in turn, found that the feeling of being seen, labeled, and accepted (even as an Other) was quite intoxicating. He straddled me, and I grabbed his muscular ass as he leaned in to give me a series of butterfly kisses on my neck that made my skin tingle.

"If you want to meet people while you're here," he said, pausing at my clavicle, "you could go to the boys' parties."

I'd heard rumors of gay all-male gatherings in Lahore, how every other week one of the smaller fish in the local fashion pond threw soirees at his home. (I know it sounds borderline sad, but Pakistanis can actually throw some pretty high-concept home celebrations. I still remember Anoushay Amjad's "Under the Sea"–themed wedding, where the dance floor was a miniature replica of a half-submerged *Titanic* next to a Styrofoam iceberg that turned out to be a prophetic metaphor for all three of her subsequent marriages.) I knew without asking that any gay parties would be purposely discreet and invitation-only, much closer to a high school bender than a Lady Gaga concert. The sofas of the living room would probably be pushed back to make room for a dance floor, destined by the end of the night to be lined with extinguished cigarette butts floating in half-empty plastic cups of cheap vodka; the host might even scatter discount disco balls around pink-tinted light bulbs to make the three dozen or so guests feel like they were in a real club. I briefly wondered what it would feel like to be in a purely gay space in Lahore, a room where I knew for a fact that everyone else was like me.

"It's not really about the talking, of course," the waiter said. Most people went to the parties for the darkrooms upstairs, pitch-black bedrooms where men had group sex under the cover of relative anonymity and plausible deniability. I would never go, of course, terrified as I was that I would run into someone who knew me or, worse, lifted my shirt.

It's exhausting, though, to hide in that depressing cubbyhole people call discretion instead of dereliction. The closest anyone in my family still came to mentioning my gayness was when my mother sighed every time a wedding invitation arrived at the house. I told myself (and was told repeatedly by others) that I was lucky my parents spoke to me at all after I came out—others had been less fortunate—and since I lived by myself now, it's not like anything was stopping me from being myself, right? My loneliness must be my choice, my fault.

"Have you noticed that you don't ever talk about sex?" Jibran once told me after I subjected him to the same rant on one of his visits to Lahore during his graduate school. The comment surprised me because I thought I spoke of nothing else.

"I mean, you talk about *being* gay," he conceded. "Like, constantly—"

"Thanks."

"Sometimes it's like a rainbow fucked a unicorn and—"

"What's your point?"

"I just meant," he said, draining the dregs of his red wine in a single gulp, "that ever since you moved back here, it's like you're in one place but your sex life is, like, something—*somewhere*—else."

"*Your* sex life is somewhere else," I muttered, fighting the reflex to inhale the pastries on the side table. He was right, of course, in that infuriating way people who are not you sometimes can be. Yes, I was out to my family and friends, but my (barely) public profile as a gay man existed in isolation, without a partner, or boyfriend, or the scantest implication that I had sex at all. I suppose my private tendencies were a sad capitulation to remaining acceptable to my family and Lahore at large. Maybe that's why I held a begrudging sense of respect for the men who were brave enough to host these gay parties. They were doing openly what I couldn't.

"You should go to one," the waiter said as he straightened the brass name tag on his polyester shirt. "People at the boys parties are . . ."

"Gay?"

"Nice," he said, laughing. He had a lovely laugh.

"I doubt they've been accused of that before."

"What I mean is," he said, combing his thick dark hair in front of the mirror, "over there it doesn't matter if you are a millionaire or office clerk, you know? Everyone is the same. Everyone wants the same thing, everyone is hiding from the same people." Sufficiently coiffed, he turned to leave. "Maybe we can go together?" He had meant to sound offhand, but I could tell he was nervous for my reply.

"Maybe," I said. I imagined us walking into the boys party, arm in arm, as the men ogled him in desire and me in envy for being so close to him. But the scene quickly shifted to the two of us at my parents' home for Sunday lunch, baking under the searing heat of my mother's scorn, my father's fear, and my sister's stares.

The biggest change about living and loving in Pakistan again was also probably the most obvious: people here looked like me. Never underestimate the power of familiarity. There is a unique strength you can draw when you see your form represented in the world around you, and those of us who are not straight and white sometimes acclimatize so well to going without it that it can be disconcerting when we are faced with ourselves again after so very long. It wasn't until I began sleeping with men from my own country that I realized how unusual it had been for me to touch a fragment of myself in another.

"By the way," he said as I led him quietly to the front door. "How much did that microwave cost you?"

There are flashes of the occult in most aspects of life in South Asia, a pervasive assumption that there is more to our existence on this planet than only that which we can see, touch, and buy. The sense of mysticism baked into the subcontinent is far, far older than Islam's presence in it and only one reason why psychics and astrologers are a big deal in Pakistan.

They routinely appear on morning TV shows, using a combination of astrology, birth charts, and the tarot to divine the futures of everyone from the latest caller to the national cricket team. The most famous of Pakistan's contemporary seers is a woman named Shafina, and that she hadn't been burned for witchcraft in the thirty years she's been reading fortunes forever surprises me. Shafina first gained infamy in the early nineties after news of her unnervingly accurate matrimonial predictions blew like a forest fire through the tinder hearts of unmarried girls and the mothers who harassed them.

The longer I stayed in Lahore, the more obsessed I became with meeting Shafina. I told myself a visit would make for a good column, but the truth is I needed reassurance. The weight of hiding so much of myself for so much of the time felt like being slowly erased from existence. Every morning I woke up depressed and angry, oppressed and unseen, wasting months of my life in fiery rages directed inward like a hot blowtorch. Hadn't I promised myself I'd do more? See more? Be more? Where did I go wrong? Maybe my mother was right after all, maybe I should have become an anesthesiologist.

The occult offered some hope of answers to these questions, or at least the promise that there was a larger plan. Perhaps that's why so many queer people—we well-moisturized few who feel so unwelcome in churches, mosques, and temples—gravitate toward the secular safety of tarot decks, birth charts, and palm readers in the first place. My mother no longer practiced divination anymore, but it was she who gave me my first tarot deck at ten (cursed pack; later found it had two tower cards and no sense of optimism) and I was already chanting spells by twelve; if something was wrong, I was as likely to be taken to a crystal healer as to a pediatrician, and I can't remember an exam I ever sat without some kind of enchanted talisman hanging around my neck to curry favor with whichever helpful god was listening. It made natural sense to me then to see a psychic to make sense of a future that felt like an unending highway to generational trauma.

"Shafina is really the most accurate one," Ma said as she excitedly thumbed through her mystical phone diary. Personal accounts varied: Some claimed her eyes turned white whenever she went into a trance; others swore that the true source of her power were the two jinns she kept locked up in one of her enchanted rings. The only common thread to her legend was that getting an appointment was nearly impossible. She had an exclusive roster of return clients that included famous politicians, athletes, actresses, socialites, and titans of industry. No one really knew how she took on new clients, but you can assume it wasn't because someone cold-called her and said, "Hey, can I come see you?"

"Hey," I said. "Can I come see you?"

I'd called from the landline out of the misplaced belief this would catch her off guard. For weeks no one picked up, until one day . . .

"Who is this?" asked a woman. Her voice sounded like a Disney mouse.

"My name is . . ." I scrambled for a lie. "Ahmed. Ahmed Khan."

"No, it's not," she said matter-of-factly.

I looked around, half expecting to see Shafina's form emerging from my laptop screen dripping well water like the girl from *The Ring*.

"But that's amazing—how on earth did you know?!"

"Caller ID. What do you want?"

"Oh. Um, well, I was hoping to come and see you. For a, you know"—I lowered my voice to a whisper in case her phone was tapped—"a *session.*"

She agreed surprisingly quickly given her reputation for exclusivity, but even seers have bills, I suppose. She quickly rattled off a time and an address and told me not to wear perfume.

"Does scent interfere with your aura?" I asked solemnly.

"Allergies," she said. "See you tomorrow."

Fifteen Pir Colony was a one-story house in a cozy suburb that, save for the small sign on the rusted gate with an eye on it, gave no indication that a psychic as famous as Shafina lived there at all. There were already several cars parked outside the home when I arrived, presumably safe under the watchful eyes of the fat security guard laying on a day bed and staring at the sky as he listened to a cricket match on his phone.

"Appointment?" he mumbled, eyes still fixed upward.

"She said to come at three."

He pointed a hairy finger toward the gate. "Door in front of the garden. No recording." He scratched his crotch as the crackling cheers of a faraway stadium roared in celebration.

I walked through the grassless garden toward an old wooden door, which opened with a cinematic creak. The room inside looked, at first glance, like a rural high school's production of *Downton Abbey*, all red velvet cushions and gold tasseled curtains. The walls were covered with prints of Arabic calligraphy or 3D pictures of Mecca, the only inexplicable exception being a poster of Dick Cheney's face in the corner with the phrase KINDNESS IS OVERRATED written across it in bright, cheerful letters.

A young girl wearing a hijab emerged from the side door and showed me into a tiny room, its walls unadorned except by triangles of flaking paint, which, under the light of the single oppressive bulb, cast dunes of shadows. The sound of flushing of water came from behind a closed door.

"Salaam!" a short woman with a pleasant face said as she emerged from the bathroom. "Come in, come in! Sorry for the delay but I had some very old clients before you. And you know how is it, *na*? *Gup shup tau* never stops! Anyway, we still have a few minutes before I have to pray. Sit!"

After all the rumors, I half hoped to meet a glamour witch with wild raven-colored hair and an affinity for kohl. Short, pink, and plump, her rosy cheeks always on the verge of a conspiratorial smile, Shafina looked like she belonged on the catalog cover of an upscale nursing home.

"Let's see what's in store for you, shall we?" She took my right hand between her palms and closed her eyes, a curiously intimate gesture for a stranger who'd just emerged from the bathroom.

"So," I asked, looking around for mysterious smoke or a shadow creature. "How does this work?"

Her eyes snapped open in my direction, but her gaze relaxed on a point behind me. She tilted her head as if trying to remember a song she'd heard and, after some tense moments of silence, burst into rapid speech, her body rocking back and forth like in prayer.

"Your life has been a disappointment to you," she said. Her voice was now clear and resoundingly deep, quite unlike her own. Gone was the mousy homemaker, in was the Cybil of Delphi.

"You are blessed in many ways by the Almighty, but little worked out the way you thought it would. It still won't. Not for some time. There are lessons you are to learn, things you are yet to experience. I do see there was a strong love that affected you in the past, a kind of . . . no." She frowned. "Not love. Infatuation." She nodded to herself. "Yes, that's it. Infatuation. And *pain*." She grimaced. "So much pain. Pain from your family, but also from within yourself. One day you will become a famous man. Paper, paper will set you free."

"Like a visa?" I asked. I still made sure to contact the immigration lawyer every six months or so with updated press clippings or letters of recommendation, the dim glow of that distant green card my sacred talisman for whenever I feared things in my life would never change.

"You will settle abroad," she said simply.

"Ok," I said. "Any timeline on that . . . ?"

"A year," she said confidently. "Year and a half, maybe. Also I see love in your future. Oh, look." She smiled at me, "You're blushing! She must be *very* pretty. What's her name?"

"I-I haven't met her yet," I said, the blind spots of her Sight now conspicuous.

She exhaled, a deep exhausted sigh. "These things are out of our hands. When they happen, how they happen, who really knows?"

"I thought you did, to be honest," I muttered.

"People think they can control kismet, but Allah works in his own perfect time. You must keep faith," she said. "Because I *do* see a great love. In fact, you'll have *many* marriages in your life."

"That doesn't bode well."

"Not everyone is meant to be with us for the whole journey," she said, and I nodded, wondering how much of her power was actually just bumper-sticker wisdom.

"My family," I asked. "Do you see them approving of my . . . my matches?"

She was quiet for some time "No," she said finally. "I'm sorry, but I see strife. You will not always be close to your family. Eventually you will . . . drift apart. They cannot see you, not for who you are." I looked down to hide the tears collecting in my eyes, and she gently raised my chin so I met her gaze once more. "Child," she said, smiling kindly, "I know you're in pain. But remember that this is all temporary. Whatever you lose comes back to you, manyfold. There will come a day when you find peace and it will have been worth it. I promise you that . . ."

She said more: I would experience a grave illness followed by a move abroad. I'd have two children, maybe three. I would have done well as a general or a dictator (knew it) and seeking truth will be more important to me than seeking riches, though those will come in time too. After leaving Pakistan I will travel back and forth quite often until one day I will settle away permanently. I may have issues with my right leg in my forties, but generally will live a long, rich, and happy life.

She let go of my hand and sank back into the chair, exhausted. As she muttered Arabic prayers to herself, the cynic smoking within me suspected that this performance of her Islamic piety was probably due to more than mere faith, but I hoped she remained safe.

"Come and see me before you move away next year," she said as I rose to leave.

"I will," I lied. "Thank you."

She shrugged, as if to say, *What more can a saint do?* "That will be five thousand rupees. No checks, cards, or torn notes, please."

On my weary search for spiritual meaning, I've visited palmists, psychics, numerologists, astrologers, gemologists, clairvoyants, wellness shamans, and more Wiccan midnight moon dances than I can legally disclose. In them I was searching for the same thing I was at Shafina's: hope. Some assurance that there was a bigger plan committed to my ultimate well-being, a confirmation that wishes work and that things do really get better. When being jostled around by the storms of anxiety, fear, and self-loathing, it can be helpful to have those kinds of fixed external points—whether predictions or prayer—that are unaffected by your chaos and beholden to a power higher than your inner demons.

"What did she say?" my mother asked me when she came over to my place for dinner the next day.

"Not much," I said.

"Oh, come *on!*" She nudged me with a smile. "She must have said *something* specific. Career? Money?" I thought of Shafina's prediction that my family would drift away. But predictions are not fact, and if there ever would come a day when she could fully accept my gayness, fully accept me, I should probably stop being so afraid to mention it in front of her.

"She did say something . . ."

"Yes?"

Fuck it.

"She said I'd have several major relationships. And children." I hadn't meant to sound defiant, but Ma fell immediately silent.

"These women can be such frauds," she said, and turned on the television. Hurt but unsurprised, I was about to retreat into the safety of a rehearsed conversation when I was hit by a sudden jolt of undiluted rage.

Enough.

What did she think her decades of disapproval would achieve? Had she not met the son she'd raised since birth? It had been a decade since I'd come out to my parents. All around the world queer people like me were out and proud. What was so inconceivable about me having relationships, love, and, yes, even a marriage one day, if not because she believed deep down that gay men—that I—didn't deserve any of those things?

"What?" Ma asked when she noticed me looking at her.

I wanted to let out a piercing scream, to shout out loud that if she forced me to choose between my happiness and her expectations, she would hurt me, yes, she would wound me, no doubt, but she would also lose me forever. But these are thoughts I can only articulate with the clarity of time and only did with the courage of a much later conviction. For in that moment, as she stared at me, all I felt was unworthy and dangerous.

"Nothing," I said.

Chapter 13

MATCHMAKER, MATCHMAKER

THE ABRACADAVERS TOOK TO DROPPING by my place unannounced most evenings after their evening strolls to interrogate me about my life. I didn't think they were trying to harm me so much as alleviate the monotony of their own stodgy lives. What harm was there in them imagining me with escorts from the red-light district or involved in an unwanted pregnancy with a politician's daughter? Given their fanatic interest whenever they saw a women visit my place, my actual truth was, I suspected, beyond them.

"She was just a friend from school," I said if they ever asked.

"You won't get married to a school friend, now, will you!"

"No," I agreed, thinking of Zariyan. "Not unless they were as pretty as you girls." At this they would throw their bald heads back and roar in postmenopausal delight.

"Naughty boy! Such a handsome, *naughty* boy . . ."

"Harpies," Tariq would snarl once they'd left, his single eye twitching in outrage. "Why is your life any of their business?!" It touched me more than I could express to see him offended on my behalf.

In the two years since Tariq had come into my life, he never once brought up the fact that men sometimes spent the night in my bed, but women never did. Often in Pakistan, hiding in plain sight is the safest place to be. But the longer I stayed, the dimmer my hopes became of ever finding an actual partner. If it hadn't happened in America, after all, what hope was there of love in Lahore?

The waiter and I kept meeting for a mutually convenient physical release devoid of any real emotional investment. We were in my bedroom when we heard a soft knock on my door.

"Yes . . . ?" I asked irritably. It was unusual for Tariq to come to my room this late.

"*Sahib*, there are some men are here." The heavy door muffled his voice but not his panic. "They say . . . they say they are from the Agency."

I bolted up. "The Agency? Are you sure?"

"They certainly look like it. You better come out. They are asking for you by name."

Once Tariq's footsteps were far enough away, I whispered quick instructions to the waiter: "Put on your clothes, keep quiet, and whatever you do, stay in this room. Try to keep away from the windows too. Do not leave unless I come back, and do not let anyone enter unless it's me. Do you understand?" He looked as scared as I felt, but nodded. The word "Agency" has pricked us both. It was like someone saying the CIA was at your door.

"I told them you were alone," Tariq whispered as we both hurried to the front gate. "There are five of them. Can't see any others, but you never know, they could be lurking around."

I'd heard stories of gangs of thieves masquerading as government agents in order to gain access to unsuspecting homes, and I vividly remember actually hoping this too was something as simple as an armed robbery. The alternative was not comforting. I stopped at the front gate, took a deep breath, summoned my fakest smile, and stepped out to do battle.

"How can I help you, officers?" I said, beaming at five men in plain clothes already closing in a tight semicircle around me.

"You live here alone?" a young man about my age asked me.

"No," I replied. "Tariq, he's my helper, he lives here too."

"And how do we know who *you* are?" Tariq interjected from behind me, his voice at least an octave deeper. His Punjabi, usually floral and soft, now felt hard as rock.

"This doesn't concern servants," an older man said with a dismissive wave of his palm. He sported a surgically trimmed mustache and wore several ornate gold rings. "Leave us."

"It's fine," I said when Tariq didn't move, careful to maintain a jovial countenance. "Tariq's a member of the household. Tell me, how can I help you officers?" I dusted my Urdu with just enough of an accent to assert an English-speaking background. It helped, I'd heard, if people from the Agency thought the BBC might miss you were you to suddenly disappear.

The older man considered me for a moment as the others waited for him to speak. It was immediately clear he was the Beyoncé of this group.

"As you may or may not know," he began in an oily drawl, "we like to keep an eye on residents in the neighborhood. The area has many VIPs living nearby, and, given your nearness to the bridge"—he gestured at the concrete structure soaring above us both—"we just had some routine questions about what you . . . do here." As he spoke, I spotted one of the Abracadavers spying down on the scene from behind the lace curtain of her first floor window.

"Of course," I said, relieved to have at least one witness looking on in case something went wrong. "How can I help?"

"What is your profession?"

"I'm a painter," I said.

"What kind of painting?" he asked. Something told me he already knew.

"Humans," I said. "People, faces, portraits, things like that."

"And what is the subject matter?"

"No subject," I lied smoothly. "Just things to decorate houses, really."

"And you"—he ruffled through his papers—"are not conducting any other business out of this house?"

"No, sir."

His chest expanded slightly. The "sir" pleased him.

"I see, I see," he said. "Well, let me be frank. We've had some reports of illicit activities in this house."

"Illicit activities?"

"People coming here at various hours of the day and night. Some very late, apparently . . ." Five sets of eyes bored into me.

"Really?" I said, feigning shock. "And who gave you these reports, if may I ask?"

The lace curtain snapped shut.

"None of your bloody business," he snarled, all pretense of amiability gone. "I'll ask you one more time: What exactly are you doing here?"

Surviving moments like these in places like that depends on calculating the calculus of power. On the one hand, you might argue, I was well within my rights to call whomever I wanted to my home at whatever time of the day or night. On the other hand, Pakistani pragmatism would retort, that doesn't count for shit here. I was standing like a plaintiff in front of five presumably armed, demonstrably unidentified men who seemed to know a lot about me. I could already tell from their mannerisms they were not from the police or the army, which probably meant that they belonged to a shadier branch of governance not often concerned with legality. Not that it mattered in the larger scheme of things. As so much else my existence in Pakistan made painfully clear, if my being gay was really the reason they were here, it was I who was illegal and not them.

But I saw no car, which meant they had come to the house on foot, and it was likely that despite their aggressive posturing, they weren't high-ranking officers so much as low-level operators sent out to do menial grunt work. That gave me an advantage because, illegal or not, I probably knew more powerful people than they did.

"School friends from the Academy come by often, if that's what you mean . . . ?" I made sure the school's name struck its target before carpet-bombing them with every brand-name power broker I could think of, and noted with grim satisfaction as their bravado changed first to hostility, then to curiosity, and finally into deference.

"Haroon *sahib*?" one of the younger men said. The rest stood still, stunned into an impressed silence by the mere mention of a government minister. "You know him?"

"His son is like my brother!" I said. He wasn't, obviously. Last I heard, Haroon Jr., a burnished turd with violent tendencies, had been living off his wife's money in London for a decade. But these men had as much chance of knowing him personally as I did of turning into a rainbow-colored tit. "You know him too?"

"Haroon *sahib* is our superior," the leader replied, exuding discomfort. "I mean, I don't personally . . . we've met, of course . . ."

"Of course."

"But I don't . . ." His subordinates stared up at him like patient pets. "Anyway, I think we're all done here, yes?"

"Yes, sir!"

"Completely done! Everything in order!"

"Thank you so much for coming by, gentleman," I said, extending a smiling handshake to each of them in turn until I reached the leader. "I feel so much safer knowing our streets are so well protected. It was such a *pleasure* to meet you." You'd think we were girlfriends leaving brunch. "I'll be sure to tell Uncle Haroon you came by . . . Mr. . . . ?"

"Javaid," he said, gripping my hand with bone-crushing enthusiasm. "Amjad Javaid. Have a good evening, sir. *Allah hafiz.*"

"*Khuda hafiz!*" I waited until they began walking up the street before exhaling.

Tariq was already bouncing on a cloud of righteous anger when I walked back inside. "Who the *hell* do they think they are? Two-bit thugs trying to intimidate God-fearing people. Don't you worry, sir, if they so much as lifted a finger to you I would have smacked them so hard even their mothers' pussies would hurt!"

"So sweet of you," I said, wincing at his vivid description. "I suppose they were just doing their job."

He grunted his disagreement. "Robbers, the lot of them! Won't leave good people alone these days. They probably came here for a bribe!"

"Good thing it didn't come to that," I said. I felt so very tired.

"Sir?" Tariq said as I walked inside.

"Hmm?"

"Agency or not," he said, "you know . . . you know you can trust me, right, sir?"

"I know," I said, placing a hand on his shoulder. "I know that. Thank you." I said goodnight and walked back into my room to find the waiter fidgeting at the edge of my bed, fully dressed and jittery.

"Why was the Agency here? What did they want with you? Who were they after?"

"They've gone," I said, reaching for a cigarette. "It was nothing. A misunderstanding."

"Is it safe for me to leave?"

I thought about the five figures outside walking slowly up the road.

"Give it ten minutes or so," I said. "Just to be sure."

"*Bhain chod*," he swore, sitting back down on the bed and rubbing his temples. "It's never safe, is it? There is always something . . ."

We didn't say another word until he left. We never met again.

Most of my friends from growing up in Pakistan lived abroad now—married to careers or spouses—and to survive my solitary life in Lahore, I joined fellow delusional Pakistanis with disposable incomes on a Sisyphean routine of visa applications and temporary escapes. Cycles of working to earn just enough money from paintings to fund a short holiday abroad to regrow my sanity, until the money or visa or both ran out, after which it was back to the heat and dust to do the whole thing over again. Even in my compounding misery I knew I was fortunate to have the means and visas to travel at all; most people in Pakistan would never leave the country in their lifetimes.

Those brief trips to cities in Europe or North America were the only times I felt safe enough to try dating in earnest (any imagined freedom in Middle Eastern cities like Dubai is as laughable as it is fictional; gay people are as safe there as a yeti in a fur shop). I was en route to London on one of these trips when a belief began to take root between the in-flight meals: If only I had the perfect bachelor to introduce to my parents (rich, successful, good-looking, all the things Lahori parents want in their sons-in-law), then maybe, just maybe, my family could finally accept us, and, on a technicality, me.

There've been a handful of moments in my life when I've become aware of a new spaciousness in my mind, not a void so much as a recently excavated expansion of consciousness waiting to be filled by the rush of newness. I felt it as a child on my way to mail off a raffle ticket that would win me a BMX bike, I felt it the first day I met Jibran, and I felt that on that trip to London, this irrepressible sense that something life-altering was about to happen.

I was at a Moroccan restaurant celebrating the birthday of an old friend named Victoria when it did.

"Is this seat taken?" From the corner of my eye, I saw a hand gesture to the vacant chair next to my lamb tagine.

"All yours," I said distractedly, still studying the cocktails menu.

"Here's hoping . . ." he said. I looked up to find a tall, freckled, and tremendously well-built white man smiling down at me. His ice-blue eyes complimented the shoulder-length white-blond hair which he kept swept up in a deliberately messy top knot.

"Sebastian," he said, extending his hand, and it took every reserve of strength I had not to spontaneously orgasm under the Moroccan arches.

"Komail," I replied, pretending not to check out his leg muscles as he clumsily squeezed the mass of himself into the tiny chair beside me. He was dressed casually—a wrinkled gray linen shirt over a pair of light khakis—but his accent made him sounded like a dialect coach for the BBC.

"Boarding school," he explained with a grimace when I asked about it. "God, how I loathed that place . . ."

"Bet you mine was worse."

"I'll take that bet," he said, sipping a whiskey. "Did you have to take cold open-air showers in the snow?"

"No," I said, reaching for the hummus. "But I was accused of blasphemy. Twice."

"Fair enough!" He laughed, hands up in surrender. "You win!"

I winked at him. "Here's hoping."

As the night went on, I felt his fingers accidentally graze mine several times under the table until, about two cocktails later, he left his hand resting on mine as he told me about his new job in London ("something boring in finance") and how he had spent the last four years as a consultant in the Middle East. "I've been to Lahore before, you know. Not as often as to Islamabad, but it's a beautiful city."

He had barely excused himself to go to the rest room when Victoria slid into his vacant seat, a bubbling champagne flute in one hand and an unlit cigarette in the other.

"You two are getting along well, I see!" she said, flinging her curtain of long red hair from one shoulder to the other.

"He's gorgeous!" I whispered. "Quick! Is he, you know . . . ?"

"Probably," she said bitterly, glaring at men's room door as if it had insulted her. "But he's never mentioned it to me."

"So how do you know?"

"Rumors," she said, taking a generous gulp from her glass. "For one, he's never hit on me. Don't roll your eyes! It's a reliable test. Also, from what I've heard, he's never had a serious girlfriend."

"Never?"

"There was that one vapid stick insect he brought to New Year's Eve when we were at uni, but that felt like more of a show. Fair warning, there is a bit of baggage."

"What kind of baggage?"

"Branded baggage. Father was a minor Swedish prince, mother was an earl's daughter. Even if he is gay, posh boys like him don't talk about it until after the will's read."

"Christ."

"Half-Jewish, I think, actually," Victoria said distractedly, twirling her now-empty glass to get the waiter's attention.

"You've met his family?"

"Met the brother once. Now *he's* definitely straight, couldn't go a minute without groping my arse. Want to say he's something in the government these days? All the arseholes are. The dad died when they were young. Sent the mother off her rocker, apparently, not that they ever got along. Nasty woman. We met her at their country house once."

"A country house?"

"I know, ridiculous! It's so big it probably has its own embassy. My mum told me that there were rumors that the father had actually—oh, shit! He's coming back. Tits up, darling! Good luck!"

"Did I interrupt?" Sebastian asked, flashing a perfect grin.

"You, Seb?" Victoria purred, rising up to kiss his cheek. "Never!" They hugged, and I watched his hand slide down the sequins of her dress to stop just above the curve of her lower back. "It's *so* good to see you! Thank heavens you're back. I was just going to tell Komail about that week you and I spent in Beirut. What was the name of that fabulous little—oh my god, Michelle?!" Victoria ran over to hug a tall glamazon in a hot pink jacket who had just entered the restaurant.

"Amazing, isn't she?" I said, watching Victoria's dress shimmer like sunlight on a wave.

I felt his fingers on my hand under the table once more. "You're amazing," Sebastian said. I turned to him.

"I need to ask you something, but I don't want to offend you . . ."

"Ask away."

"I wanted to ask if . . . well, are you . . . ?" I pressed his hand, and let the question hang between us.

Sebastian squeezed me hand back, and nodded once.

He insisted on walking me to the tube station after dinner. We strolled hand in hand under the glowing pools of streetlights through chilly London, and as I held him close to me, I couldn't shake the strange presence of fate between us. "This is me," I said, stopping at the tube entrance. He pulled me roughly into his arms for a deep kiss that we held until a couple of neighborhood teenagers playfully hooted at us.

"Come back with me," he whispered in my ear. He tasted like cloves and vanilla.

"Yes."

We stumbled into his apartment still kissing, shedding more clothes the closer we got to his bed.

"You're beautiful," he said, sucking on my nipple. "So fucking beautiful."

I spent that night in his one-bedroom apartment, as I did every night for the rest of my trip. Laughing, fucking, reading, being.

Indecently soon, it was time for my flight back to Lahore. "Stay on in London," he said to me.

"But my sublet ends tomorrow," I replied, somewhat lamely.

"So?" he said, sitting up in the bed naked. "Stay here with me. We've practically been living together for weeks now. I know you have to go back to Lahore, I *do* know that. But . . . well, this doesn't happen to me very often."

"Me neither," I said.

"Just one more week. Please?"

His expression was so earnest that for a moment I saw exactly what he must have looked like as a child.

"Of course I'll stay," I said, and laughed as he jumped up and down on the bed in excitement.

A week became a month. A month became two. I fell in love.

"It's not as frightening as it looks," Sebastian assured me as we drove down the mile-long driveway toward what he described as "Mum's place" but looked like an enchanted castle from a German nightmare. Our car zoomed through an ornate wrought iron gate flanked by pillars with the words CHANCE HOUSE elegantly carved into them, but everything from the stone gargoyles to the spiral turrets suggested the building's overbearing grandeur was anything but accidental.

"It *is* just us this weekend?" I asked for the third time as we drove past the acres of manicured gardens that surrounded the manor. It had just rained (it's always just rained in England), leaving the grounds that vibrant bright shade of sap green that makes British period movies so addictive.

"Just us," he said. "I know it's a bit of a trek for your last weekend, but I really wanted you to see it before you left. It felt, I dunno, important."

I reached up to tuck a stray lock of his hair behind his ear, and he grabbed my hand to kiss my fingers. "Thank you for coming."

"Thank you for bringing me."

Sebastian turned the car in a wide arc around an ornate stone fountain before coming to a stop on the gravely driveway. I took a deep, steadying breath as we got out in the shadow of an imposing limestone entrance bearing a weathered coat of arms; the air smelled like mint and pine. The heavy wooden front doors were unlocked and led into an enormously grand entrance hall at least three stories high and capped at the top with a magnificently gilded Pantheon-like dome; in front of us, an old stone staircase soared upward before splitting off at the top landing toward different wings of the building. The walls were studded with several scallop-edged niches that displayed marble busts and statuary, some of them glowing silver under the bright rays of sun beaming down through the oculus at the center of the dome. Around them, portraits of old white people in fabulous wigs competed for attention with large landscapes and even larger woven tapestries; scattered around the ground floor were various seating arrangements, and every available flat surface was crowded with Chinese vases, jade plates, and gilt-framed photographs.

"What do you think?" he asked.

"Bit small," I said and the sound of his laughter echoed off the veined marble floor.

"I thought I heard the sound of trouble!" A plump English woman of about sixty emerged from a side door. Her white hair was swept up in a tight bun, and she wore a cream cardigan and thick blue trousers under a well-used gardening apron.

Sebastian strode over and lifted the woman up in his arms and off the floor.

"Seb, put me down this instant!" she cried out, but giggled as he twirled her in midair.

"Good to see you, old bird," he said, carefully putting the lady down on the floor again. "Komail, this is Nanny Hillary, the woman who raised me."

She turned slightly pink at his description but wiped her palms on her apron and extended a hand to me.

"Always nice to meet a new friend of Sebastian's," she said.

"Pleasure's all mine," I said. "Thank you for having me in your home."

"Oh, bless you, sweet thing," she said with a little chortle. "I'm just the housekeeper! But you're very welcome here, very welcome indeed."

"She's everything here," Sebastian said, rubbing her shoulder.

"Your mother will be happy to see you," Nanny Hillary said, looking at him with an expression I couldn't read. "She was so worried when you didn't come down for August."

"I thought Mother was in Paris," Sebastian said. His voice sounded tight.

"Weather wasn't to her liking," Nanny Hillary said. "She'll be here later this afternoon." Several moments of silence. "Anyway," Nanny went on, "you boys go settle in and I'll have some tea and cakes fixed up. Oh, what a frightful journey it must have been! You know, dear," she said, hooking her arm into the crook of my elbow for support as she led me up the main stairs, "in the old days before the new paved road was built, we had to jump on a cart at the train station. Oh, and how those things would—"

Nanny Hillary chattered on in an uninterrupted monologue of polite nothingness as we navigated through the labyrinthine hallways of Chance House, but I noticed Sebastian's face harden with every step. I was put in a guest room decorated with a frilly four-poster bed and cream paisley wallpaper that overlooked a bucolic lake, not far from Sebastian's old room, which was large, peacock blue, and still plastered with faded posters of *Buffy the Vampire Slayer*. We spent the rest of the afternoon exploring the house. He showed me the secret door in the library that opened by pressing on a sconce, and the nook in the medieval-era kitchen where he would hide as a child to escape homework. We kissed under the oak tree he used to climb as a child.

At one point Sebastian had to take a work call, and I found myself alone in the "Hunting Room," a large and frightening study whose plush burgundy walls were mounted with a disturbing number of snarling taxidermy tiger heads. Next to each were framed sepia photographs showing old white men (presumably Sebastian's relatives) surrounded by scores of Indian attendants, all posing unsmilingly in front of the splayed carcasses of these once-majestic animals. Most of the photographs had places and dates scrawled on them in slanted writing—"*Bengal 1909*," "*Jodhpoor 1918*." As I studied them, I wondered how much of his family's wealth was built on the untold riches extracted from the Indian subcontinent. *How different would home be today*, I wondered while looking at the brown faces of my compatriots in the photographs, *had we not been looted and plundered for centuries so that these pale people on this frigid little island could maintain the delusion that they owned the world?* But Sebastian came back, and seeing his face forced the thought out of my mind, leaving me feeling once again like the colonized heroine of a Merchant Ivory movie (with better indoor plumbing). *How happy my parents would be for us*, I thought as we walked toward the Chinese drawing room.

Sebastian's mood continued to darken the closer we got to dinner. I'd yet to meet anyone from his family, or indeed anyone from his life who actually knew him well in the months we had spent together. If I asked why he didn't socialize with his friends more, he'd shrug. "I'd rather spend time with you." I worked hard to accept his need to be in the closet everywhere but our bed. His discretion felt so familiar to me, a twin to my own in Pakistan.

"Listen," he said, pausing behind a stone pillar on our way down to dinner. He looked very worried. "I just want to say that I'm sorry."

"Sorry for what?"

"I really didn't think my mother would be here." I knew he wasn't close to his mother, and, from what he said, the feeling was mutual.

"That's OK," I said. "I'm great with parents!"

"The thing is," he went on, staring at the old Persian rug beneath us. "I haven't . . . I mean, she doesn't . . ." He bit his lip.

"She doesn't know about us," I said.

"She doesn't know about *me*," he corrected.

"All right," I said. "I understand. I'm a friend this weekend."

Relief swept over him in an obvious wave; his shoulders relaxed, his forehead unknotted, and his smile flickered back to life. "It's like we're *made* for each other," he said, and as I sank deeper into his kiss, I let myself believe it.

When we entered the opulent bloodred dining room overlooking the front garden, his mother was already seated at the head of an imposingly long table. She was a frighteningly thin woman, with deep-set eyes, high cheekbones, and an even higher gray bouffant. She wore a large beetle-shaped diamond broach, an elegant black evening dress, and a look of deep resentment.

"Mother," Sebastian said curtly as we approached. She raised a cheek toward him and he leaned down to peck it, quickly. Her eyes never left me.

"A new face?" she said.

"Pleasure to meet you," I said, flashing my brightest smile.

"Komail," Sebastian said. "This is my mother, Flora. This is Komail. He's . . . we're friends."

A flicker of irritation at the mention of her first name. "Lady Chancery," she said, extending a bony, bejeweled hand toward me. "Welcome to Chance House. Had I known Sebastian was bringing

one of his friends over, I'd have made better preparations for dinner."
She gestured vaguely around the forty-seat table.

"Thank you for having me," I said, sitting down to her right. The
ensuing silence stretched out long enough that I could hear the ticking
of the grandfather clock.

"You have a lovely home," I finally added, looking up at a rather
famous Spanish painting hanging directly behind her.

"That's nice to hear," she replied, snapping out a starched white
napkin and laying it carefully across her lap. "It's a leaky old thing
but we do love it here, don't we, Seb?" Sebastian reached over for the
decanter of red wine. A young woman appeared from a side door
wearing the kind of black-and-white maids uniform I've only ever seen
in old movies. She smiled at me and began ladling out cream of mush-
room soup into our delicate china bowls. Lady Chancery went on:
"Of course, Damian—that's my eldest—is off at our board meeting in
Zurich this week, so it all feels a bit empty now. I had hoped to finish
some reading this weekend, but guests are always fun too!" she said,
smiling at me as if to say, *Do be a dear and die in your sleep tonight.*

I smiled back. If this bleached raisin thought she could scare me
off armed with nothing but archival Chanel and a discount Disney villain impersonation, she had another thing coming. Passive-
aggressive dinners with bitter matriarchs are the center of my confront
zone. Strap in, Countess.

Dinner passed in a volley of barbed compliments. Sebastian spoke
very little throughout but his eyes darted to his mother's every so
often as if waiting for a final attack. It arrived as we ate the last
crumbs of the lemon cheesecake. "Your English is terribly good,
Komail. How is that?"

"Mother," Sebastian warned.

"What? His English *is* good," Lady Chancery said. "It's quite an
accomplishment! Where did you say you grew up again, dear?"

"Lahore," I replied. "It's a city in Punjab."

"Oh, we know the Poonjab well!" she said. "The family has quite a storied history in the subcontinent, you know." Not my family or our family. The family.

"Yes, I saw the corpses earlier today," I said. At least Sebastian laughed.

"The tigers in the hunting room were shot by my great-grandfather," she said a fraction too loudly, but then modulated her pitch, "Mostly Bengal, of course. A present from the ruler. Dear little thing. We're still friends with the family. You people have some good country out there."

"He's not Bengali," Sebastian said. "He's from Lahore." He looked as livid as his mother did pleased.

"Of course," she whispered, curving her mouth into a impersonation of a smile. "My mistake."

There was a roar of car engines from outside. Through the windows, I spotted three black SUVs come to screeching stop near the front door. Some minutes later a short, pudgy blond man walked into the dining room. He greeted his mother first and then nodded at Sebastian.

"Damian," Lady Chancery said to her eldest son. "This is Sebastian's new friend. From Pakistan."

The brothers shared the same shade of white-blond hair, but Damian's was, like the rest of him, short and spiky. He offered me a perfunctory handshake and, after some moments of unenthusiastic conversation about my journey, gestured at the door leading to the adjoining drawing room. "If you wouldn't mind, we have some family business to discuss," he said. It took me some moments (and a glance at Lady Chancery's face) to realize he wanted me to leave them alone at the table. I smiled at Sebastian to make sure he knew I wasn't upset and thanked them for dinner. The drawing room next door was predictably large but surprisingly cozy, divided into several separate seating areas and dotted with shaded lamps. I had barely finished performing my Hercule Poirot monologue in front of the roaring fireplace when Sebastian stormed inside looking absolutely livid. He was alone.

"We're leaving tomorrow morning," he announced. "Come on, let's go up. I don't want to spend another *second* with them!"

"What happened?" I asked. He refused to say more, but it wasn't hard to guess. Lady Chancery was not a fan.

It didn't matter. After years of false starts and threadbare dreams, I finally had a boyfriend! He was smart, beautiful, worldly, charming, sexy, kind, and even the omnipresent despair of my manboobs seemed to evaporate in his presence (cutting carbs helped). Sebastian was everything I'd been waiting for in a boyfriend. If life were a Jane Austen novel (and a dispiriting number of South Asians believe it should be), I had just bagged the book's best bachelor.

And in the comical way that fate sometimes works, I returned from London after those first months with Sebastian to find I had been included in a list of eligible bachelors of Pakistan, an unprovoked honor that had brought with it an entirely unwelcome level of national scrutiny into my otherwise subterranean love life. A young editor had actually asked me to appear in an artist's profile some months before, which I'd agreed to because every bit of press would help for my green card application. But the story had switched directions in my absence, and what started out as a profile of young creatives morphed without my knowledge into full-page photo of me in the Sunday papers next to percentages ranking my face, body, and talent in numbers I've only ever told my second therapist.

Suddenly strangers online were not only aware I existed but very interested in who I was dating, which, particularly given Sebastian's feral need for discretion, was very inconvenient. I was having lunch with my only straight school friend from the Academy at a newly opened Korean restaurant when he revealed even he had heard rumors about my sex life. I hadn't really been listening (there are only so many times one can say "wow" to pictures of a two-year-old) until:

" . . . but I told her that I know for a fact you don't have a twin brother."

"I'm sorry," I said, suddenly alert now. "What was that?"

Turns out that his aunt had held court at a recent luncheon to inform people that my father had not one son, but two. One was the nice young man who had moved back to Lahore to get married (presumably the version of me eating Korean food), while the other, well, he was "a gay," a shameful mistake that had run away with a man years ago and now performed five nights a week at a Las Vegas show.

"Las Vegas?" I said as the waiter set another steaming plate of rice down on the table. "Caesars or off-strip?"

"She didn't specify."

"Who cares what they say?" Sebastian said when I vented to him later about the indignity. "I for one feel honored to be dating Pakistan's most eligible bachelor!"

"Third," I said grimly. I felt a flash of irritation that Sebastian, who six months into our relationship still refused to hold my hand publicly, even in the comparative safety of Europe, could be so dismissive of my fears. But the memory of his face softened my anger. "I miss you," I sighed. "I wish we were together."

"Come back," he whispered.

"You know I can't, not until the new visa comes."

"Fucking visas," he said.

"Says the prince with a Swedish passport . . ."

The results from my debut on the heterosexual meat market were swift and intense. Unknown aunties began striking up unsolicited conversations at weddings and dinners, invariably making up an abrupt excuse to leave me in the company of their usually young and always single daughters. The girls and I would lock eyes in mutual apology before stalking off to different ends of the hidden bar, but it was amazing how suddenly helpful society at large had become in finding me someone to date now that they assumed I was straight. The harder they tried, the more jealous I became of the casual entitlement with which these parents insinuated themselves into their kids' lives; jealous too of their kids who got to live their romantic lives openly over family dinners and cheese platters without fear of shame, rebuke, or violence. I understand, of course, that women in Pakistan feel a crushing pressure all unto themselves, but my point is that it makes a huge difference in the probability of finding a mate if the machinery of courtship works for you rather than against you. I couldn't really imagine an aunty waddling up to me to brag about how wonderful her son was, and wouldn't it be nice if we caught a matinee of *Guys and Dolls* together.

I jest, of course.

They don't have matinees in Pakistan.

There were other rumors too: I was in Lahore because I was secretly running from the law in the US, I was married to a Spanish prostitute, I made porn in San Francisco, I was a drug dealer for foreign diplomats in Islamabad. The narrative arc they came up with for why I moved out of my parents' home was positively biblical. Essentially what they were all just trying to understand was how exactly I fit into their world. Why did someone like me, so decidedly different, dare to come back at all? Aren't types like me meant to self-banish? I couldn't be gay because that doesn't happen here. Gay people run away and make porn and do shows in Vegas.

As if I had the discipline for that kind of diet.

Chapter 14

NOW A WARNING?!

I N THE LATE SUMMER, WHEN Lahore's skies darken into swirls of heavy gray, it can get so humid that the air itself feels like a water balloon only a pinprick away from bursting. That sense of imminent doom is, on reflection, ubiquitous in Pakistan, but it feels far nicer in rainy weather.

There are few things in this world I like less than sweat stains (except spin classes; oh, how I loathe optimistic cycling). On the cursed days I forayed outside into the heat of the monsoons, my sweat stains would fan out from under my arms with the unfashionable urgency of a Rorschach ink blot. I tried everything in my power to stop the flood before it reached my nipples (by which time most wars are lost), but nothing worked; toilet paper turned to pulp, talcum powder to paste, and even carefully laid swathes of paper towels eventually migrated of their own accord, creating folds and ridges far too fantastical to be explained away as mere "bloating."

"You're doing it wrong," Victoria once advised me with her usual air of authority. "Menstrual pads. *Always* go for the pads. Trust me, if they can absorb all that blue water in the TV ads, they can deal with your pits."

The constant threat of public intrusions into my personal life slowly eroded my sense of safety until I felt as diminished as a stone made small by an unrelenting river. Sebastian's paranoia about being outed meant I felt I must keep his secret for both of us. I didn't talk about my relationship to my family (not that they asked) or post pictures of us online, so art remained the only language available to work through all I couldn't say out loud. Painting particularly, already a step removed from the bald declarative power of words, allowed me the space for all sorts of conversations that Pakistani society avoided on principle. Ever aware of the religious violence that coursed through Pakistan, I often relied on the crutch of plausible deniability. Everyone did. Drawing a male nude might put me in a tricky position, but proving in a court of law that making it meant I was gay myself was nearly impossible. Not that the art scene was without its own depressing trials for the soul, as I found out after a gallerist called me up one Sunday afternoon.

"There's a problem," she said without preamble. "Your painting has been possessed by evil spirits."

This was not on the list of things I thought a gallerist might say to me.

"I don't know how to respond to that," I replied honestly, and waited for an explanation.

One of the larger pieces in my latest show was an oil painting I had made that imagined what the many, many wives of the prophet might have looked like had Annie Leibovitz photographed them for a *Vanity Fair* cover. It was large, it was blue, it was fabulous. After a short-lived but exceedingly validating bidding war, the piece sold to a businessman with a growing art collection. The downside of making art inspired by religious mythologies in a place like Pakistan was that, as I would soon realize, people can confuse art with artifact. And so it happened that six months after buying the piece, the businessman's life crumbled around him like a flaky tart: his wife left him, his companies failed, his money evaporated, and he lost everything except his weight, which he doubled. He traced this embarrassment of misfortunes directly back to the acquisition of my painting, which, he was now convinced beyond all doubt, was possessed by evil jinns. Or Satan.

"I'm the reason he put on weight?"

"One of them," the gallerist said. "Stop laughing! It's not a joke. He really wants to burn the painting."

"Burn it?"

"He says he'll wait until after the exorcism, of course—"

"Of course."

"—because he needs to get rid of spirits living inside it first."

"How many?"

"Two. Look, I know this all sounds ridiculous, but it could be worse."

"How?" I cried.

"At least he paid in cash."

Already formulating a punchy version of the story in my head to tell my friends abroad, I could imagine my art professors chortling at the surrealism of actually being accused of creating the younger, meaner sister of the picture of Dorian Gray. How charming! How backward! How *Best Exotic Marigold Hotel*!

But the truth is I loved that painting, and that it could be held hostage to the whims of an emotional overeater afraid of inter-dimensional fairies was a demoralizing notion no matter how good of a story it made. *This* was the reality of being a working artist in a place in Pakistan. What was the point? I even tried to buy the painting back from him, but the businessman refused because "spirits don't like to be moved." After weeks of fruitless negotiations, he eventually agreed not to burn the painting on the condition that the piece undergo a cleansing ritual and never be displayed in public again. In related news, did you know that exorcists offer group discounts?

I ran into my superstitious patron at another art show some months later. We locked eyes across a sculpture made of roadkill ("found anatomy," the artist called it), but he hid behind a shrimp platter to avoid me. I was half-tempted to confront him with my impersonation of the girl from *The Exorcist* but refrained. For all his religious blustering, in the end he sold the piece on to someone else for five times as much as he paid for it. But also, I was the guest of a woman named Honey, a wealthy bleach-blond art collector from Karachi, and thought better of embarrassing her in public.

Honey and I were there to see a group show by recent graduates from the local college of art. I'd been excited, particularly since they were showing work by a trans male artist. Their paintings were of various young men posing naked in bedrooms; some splayed on chairs, others sprawled on beds, all of them charmingly naked and unmistakably homoerotic. But as we meandered around the former living room that had been expensively remodeled to resemble a concrete white box, Honey got upset.

"What I don't understand is *why* they have to talk about it so much," she said as we walked around the room. "I mean, I don't go shouting about *my* sexuality from the rooftops, do I? Whatever happens in your own bedroom is fine, but why be so grotesquely public about it all?"

The sting of her comment winded me.

"*Be* with whoever you want to," she went on, leaning in to study a particularly large set of testicles. "I'm not against anything, *of course*. But what's the point of talking about your sex life so openly? Aren't some things meant to be private? What's happened to dignity?"

I'd heard versions of the argument before, all of them circling the same dark drain of disgust: Why do you have to exist so very much? Interestingly, nearly all my inquisitors were self-professed Pakistani liberals, casual supporters of whatever value system let them throw their weekend benders in relative peace. Implicit in Honey's question was the assumption that we—all the beleaguered liberals stuck in this rapidly collapsing foxhole—were in this together. Maybe that's why the betrayal hurt so much. Circumstance had deluded me into thinking we were on the same side, but the truth was we were only running from the same enemy.

As the twice-divorced, straight daughter of an absurdly wealthy man, Honey never worked a day in her life unless she chose to. She probably felt no fear in telling her parents when she wanted to get married the first time, nor indeed when she decided to do the whole thing all over again with a new dress, a new groom, a new wedding, and a new kid. Why was it so difficult for her to give others the space that she took so freely?

"It's not like women have it easy!" she muttered, slightly appalled at my reading of her life.

"I never said they did," I said. "I'm a feminist. I just don't understand—"

"I'm so sorry to interrupt you." A kind-looking old woman wearing a pink *kameez* tapped me on the shoulder. "But I think you dropped this."

She opened her wrinkled, liver-spotted hand to reveal a wad of white . . . was it paper?

"Oh," I said, studying the mass. "Thank you, I'll just . . ."

The three of us stared down as the white clump unfurled in her palm like a rare blooming orchid.

"What is . . . ?"

"Is that a . . . ?"

"It can't be . . ."

The answer hit us simultaneously, a slow, mortifying realization that the mass wasn't paper at all, but a moist menstrual pad that had dislodged itself from my armpit during one of my wilder hand gestures.

"See?" I said to Honey, reaffixing the menstrual pad underneath my armpit as the granny shuffled away as fast as her walker would let her. "Feminist."

I had been in Lahore for over four years by 2014, but trauma works like time in Narnia, so it felt like centuries. Grueling slogs through hundred-degree summers, the daily specter of violence and hours without electricity can wear out even the most glamorous soul. It didn't help that I was responsible for my own bills in a place where most of my peers lived with their families. Despite my horror at familial cohabitation, I envied friends who had to do little more than tell someone that the kitchen had blown up for it to be fixed by sundown, while I had to negotiate with tradesmen in crowded alleys for weeks to get so much as a toaster repaired. Sebastian listened to me complain during our nightly conversations, nearly always offering to fly me out to see him so I didn't have to put up with any of it, which was sweet but rarely helpful. His world of members-only clubs and evenings at expensive restaurants was comically far from my daily reality of man-eating mosquitoes and nosy neighbors. I felt embarrassed trying to explain to him that, as a working artist entirely reliant on my paintings to eat, it made me upset to receive monthly bills demanding hundreds of dollars for electricity that only appeared with the frequency of a reluctant chanteuse. Summers in South Asia, I want to stress, are profanely hot, but when running a single air conditioner can set you back $940 a month (bill for July 2014), my anger ran hotter.

It was—is—important to me to acknowledge that being gay didn't automatically preclude me from being a Pakistani any more than being a Shia, agnostic, feminist, liberal, or sane did. Any one of these things could be weaponized to eradicate me, cast me as other, and put me on the wrong side of the anonymous many. I'd seen as much all around me: parents of friends murdered in cold blood, school children abducted off the street for ransom or worse, journalists assassinated at traffic stops. The relative safety of any class privilege was more hope than fact; everyone knew that if they wanted to get you, they could, whoever "they" were at the time. For a while, the bombings in Lahore became so frequent it felt like one had the same chances of being killed for buying fruit at the wrong time as for being an apostate.

My unhappiness didn't make sense to me. Sure, my family issues were less than saccharine, but I was earning a living from my art, lived on my own terms in my own place, and even had a boyfriend waiting for me to visit him. Everything in my life was a product of not only my choice but my fight. Why, then, wasn't I happy? Now that I'd made my life in two rooms under a bridge, what was next?

Sebastian was my answer, and I ignored anything that suggested otherwise: like how he abruptly hung up our phone calls if he ever ran into someone on the street he knew, how he never let me take pictures of us together, how he always avoided holding my hand in public; his fundamental belief that being gay and being himself were fundamentally incompatible and always would be. I thought instead of how he arranged for roses to be delivered to me on Valentine's Day, his coded notes of affection, how he fell asleep every night listening to true crime podcasts, his kindness, and his smile. I molded my schedule and strained my budget to its absolute limit to find stolen moments together whenever I could. To pay for the trips, I began taking on private commissions, mostly portraits of society ladies and their firstborn grandchildren. The work felt meaningless as art, but I had been waiting for years to fall for someone, and now that I had, painting someone's baby seemed like a small price to pay to be with him. One fall evening we were in Paris together, and Sebastian took me for a long walk along the shimmering Seine. We'd had some red wine with dinner, and as he nuzzled my neck in the yellow light of a streetlamp after he was sure we were alone, I remember thinking: *I don't need a green card. Why would I be anywhere he is not?*

Later that year, around November, once the chilly smog of winter finally arrived in Lahore, I arranged to surprise Sebastian in London for his thirtieth birthday. I'd been busy painting in Lahore for my next show, but he'd been insistent that I come visit him whenever we spoke, angrily enough in our last few conversations that I just assumed he missed me a lot. I made a plan on the flight to Heathrow: We'd go on a walk along the River Thames, pause at our favorite hidden brick alcove, and there, in the light of a setting sun, I would tell him I loved him and propose we spend our lives together. The prospect of legal union didn't entice me so much as the legitimacy the declaration conferred on our relationship. He was everything I thought my *Fawlty Towers*–watching family wanted in a son-in-law, and I imagined their approval when he one day came to my parents' home for a dinner of Kabuli pulao and roast chicken. Maybe now my mother would finally approve. He'd studied history at university before pivoting to finance (posh Englishmen can always pivot), which meant Dad would love him too. On and on I went, erecting an entire scaffolding of dreams for an imagined future without once checking whether the ground beneath me was stable enough to support it.

I knew something was off the moment Sebastian opened his door. His ice-blue eyes were bloodshot, his white-blond hair filthy and matted. His one-bedroom apartment, usually tolerably messy, now looked like a tornado had just passed through it. Clothes were strewn around, tables legs broken, paintings slashed, the mirror we bought together at a Brick Lane thrift shop shattered to stardust on the floor. He ignored my many questions, his eyes shifty and unfocused as he jumped from one subject to the next. He insisted we go out to dinner immediately, and on the way, he walked far too quickly. As we spoke, I noticed he had forgotten entire months of our time together, but it wasn't until we sat down at the table that I realized he was having full-fledged conversations with invisible people around him.

The next day, he threw our Thai takeout in the trash unopened because he thought I was trying to poison him. "I don't know what's happening to me," he said to me through tears in one of his rare moments of lucidity, but a shadow quickly passed over his eyes and he resumed muttering numbers to himself, lost.

Things got much worse. His refusal to sleep made him more erratic as each night passed. He stopped eating or drinking, and survived on a diet of cigarettes and Diet Coke. I tried to manage him as best I could, to wrestle him back from the clutches of whatever demon had possessed the man I loved. One night I woke up from a noisy, shallow sleep to find an empty bed. In a panic, I followed the carnage of broken furniture out onto the apartment's small balcony overlooking the London skyscrapers. I saw Sebastian standing on the wrong side of the railing, his hands holding the bar behind him as he leaned dangerously forward, his blue silk pajamas fluttering in the icy wind, his cold bare feet mere inches away from a twelve-story drop. I asked what he was doing, and he shouted out that he wanted to fly across Big Ben like Peter Pan. He moved to take a step and I screamed.

"I *told* you I can fly, silly!"

It took half an hour to persuade to climb back inside. The moment he did, I barricaded him inside his bedroom and ignored the mad screams and thuds as he flung objects at the door. I didn't want to call the police, and so took his phone and scrolled through to find anyone I could to help us. Anyone, I prayed, but her.

Lady Chancery picked up on the third ring and remained utterly silent as I explained what was happening to her son.

"I don't know what to do," I finished.

"Thank you for calling," she said. Her voice was calm and entirely without emotion. "Make sure he's presentable, would you? Damian will be there shortly." It was only much later that I found out how pervasive severe schizophrenia was in their family, how their father had committed suicide when Sebastian was five by flinging himself off the tallest turret at Chance House because of the same cruel disease that lies dormant in an otherwise healthy person before manifesting in their late twenties to destroy their mind. Twenty minutes later Damian barged through the front door of the apartment accompanied by two security guards and a man in a white coat. As the guards wrestled Sebastian into submission inside the bedroom, he told me Sebastian had been prescribed serious medication for the illness some years ago, but clearly he hadn't been taking the pills of late. Surely I had noticed something? He'd already been fired from his finance job, crashed his car, and physically harmed a friend. The family would have to admit him to a private institution that could take better care of him; there was no other option now.

"What can I do to help?" I asked, trying to process the avalanche of information.

A smirk of incredulity passed across his face.

"Nothing," Damian said, as if it were the most obvious thing in the world. "This is a family matter."

I'm not family. Of course I'm not.

The doctor gave Sebastian a powerful tranquilizer, and together we carried his limp body to the elevator and down into a waiting car. After making a begrudging promise to update me as to Sebastian's progress, Damian asked me to please vacate the apartment by the next day. "The cleaners need to get in, you see," he said.

And as I watched the sleek black car speed Sebastian away from me, I knew in my heart we would never be together again. I had no resources to care for him, and no visa that would allow me to try. It had to be his family, and whatever unsaid words remained between us, I was not his family and never would be. I waited until I was back in Lahore to cry. I woke up two weeks later, on the morning of my own thirtieth birthday, to a life I despised. The thing about having lived out your "youth" is that a very harsh, very honest part of your mind inevitably turns around with a cigarette dangling from its bitter mouth to ask in a Russian accent: "Vos zat eet?"

I waited weeks and then months for any news from Sebastian's family, but nothing. I could imagine what they thought of me well enough: a shameful sidepiece, a troublesome bit of Sebastian's unfortunate sexual perversion that now refused to go away.

I retreated into a cancerous depression, a hard, metallic flagellation I saw as comeuppance for my own weaknesses. I slept till dusk and stayed up till dawn, lost in a haze of cigarettes, anonymous sex, painting, and desolation. I didn't matter that I had lost so much weight that for the first time in living memory my manboobs had receded into square planes of muscle. It didn't matter that I was selling my work for more than I ever had before. Nothing mattered. I deserved to be here, I told myself with every self-hating thought, alone and unloved.

Keeping the secret of our relationship still felt like some feeble proof that it had happened at all, which is perhaps why I found myself unable to talk to anyone around me. Like most things we believe to protect ourselves, this was a lie. I was not alone, despite how it felt, and I knew I was not unloved, except by myself. But I also knew that the blame was not only mine to bear. It belonged to Sebastian's inability to treat our relationship without shame. It belonged to his family that had forced him to do it. It belonged to my family who refused to ask me any details of my love life lest they be forced to confront something they didn't want to. It belonged to a society that refused to talk about my love in anything but embarrassed whispers or hostile threats. It belonged to the Muslim world that demonstrated daily how unsafe it was for anyone to be different. It belonged to the West that first caused, then denied, and then usurped those differences to further its own imperialist ends. My depression belonged to everyone, the inevitable result of a lifetime spent being told by both words and silence that my love was a shameful thing years before I ever dared to love at all.

My time with Sebastian convinced me that any attempt to integrate my sexuality into my family, life in Pakistan, or indeed anywhere, would not only be difficult but impossible, no matter how far back in the closet I made my home.

Munda666 says: *Pics?*

I sent off the usual collection. A pouting selfie along with a picture of my shirtless torso taken in flattering lighting after a very successful stomach flu, a bottle of shampoo placed strategically to hide the deflated flap of loose stomach skin I'd never managed to kill off.

Munda666 has blocked you.

My first thought was what would happen if the pics got out. *Whatever*, I reasoned, flinging my phone down on the bed. *I've got someone coming over anyway. Who needs Munda666?*

He said he was a low-ranking officer in the navy, but when he drove into my driveway in a shiny new car, something told me he'd lied. We'd hooked up once before, an awkward encounter where he had asked me to hump the space between his thighs in a disease-free approximation of intercourse. But pickings were slim in Lahore, and to find someone attractive who regularly used deodorant was enough of a reason to meet again.

"Don't worry about him," he said, nodding at his driver, who was already reversing down the road. "He has no clue."

I nodded and locked the front gate behind us, the metal handle still cold from the winter breeze. He followed me into the house, through my studio littered with red splotches and gold flecks, and into my bedroom, where we immediately started to kiss. His body was the latest in a string of attempts I'd made to forget about Sebastian, about me, about life. About twenty minutes in, he paused and began rummaging through the pockets of his discarded jeans. I watched the sinews of his leg muscles ripple from the bed.

"Ah!" He raised a tiny brown glass bottle in the air. "Got it."

"What's that?"

"Ever had G?"

"No," I replied, silently annoyed that he didn't take the no-drugs part of my profile seriously. He offered me a sip, but I refused, and he shrugged before taking a generous gulp himself and returning to bed. This happened four more times in the next ten minutes, until, midkiss, I saw his eyes roll back into his skull.

"Hey," I said, shaking his face gently. His lids were heavy and close to sleep. "Are you OK?"

He replied by vomiting over my bedspread and passing out over the box of condoms, lifeless and limp as a dead cat. Instinct told me to drag him under a cold shower to shock him awake, but he only slumped over onto the wet bathroom tiles. It wasn't until I tried to lift him up again that I noticed he wasn't breathing, and backed into my bedroom screaming with symphonic panic of a horror film victim. That's where I saw his phone light up with a flurry of messages, and two things occurred to me fairly quickly.

One: Tariq would be coming back any minute now from his grocery run to discover a naked dead man in my shower. Two: The naked dead man in my shower was definitely an army officer whose impatient subordinates were on their way over right now to pick him up.

It can be strange for overthinkers to witness the clarity of thought a true crisis can inspire. Vast highways of noise shut down until all that's left is an empty expressway of numb self-preservation. Next thing I remember is smoking a cigarette as I stared coldly at his limp form. There was no way for me to explain his presence here to the police, nor to prove that I had nothing to do with the drugs in his system. As far as the police would be concerned (and Pakistanis spend a lot of time and money making sure the police are never concerned), I had a dead, naked, gay army officer in my home in a country where an army officer shouldn't, ideally, be any of those things.

His phone lit up again. Emergency meeting. They were ten minutes away. I closed my eyes, and for a brief moment the villains of *Cruel Intentions* began whispering to me.

Get rid of the body.

But where?

Away from the house.

Where could I bury him? The banks of the Canal? Do I even own a shovel? Perhaps no one would notice if I transported him somewhere far away in my own car, *Weekend at Bernie's*–style? But even if I could get past the five army checkpoints on the way to the outskirts of the city, what then? A body with a rank can't simply disappear. Can it?

If they find you, you are dead. Not metaphorically, not symbolically. Quite literally dead.

The sound of a wet cough interrupted my sociopathy.

"W-wh . . ." He tried to lift his head but passed out again. I collapsed on the tiled floor next to him, gasping in sheer relief. Eventually I reached over, propped him up against the shower wall, and slapped him with the abandon of a soap opera matriarch.

"Wake up!"

Nothing. More slaps.

"Wake! Up!"

His eyes jolted open, pupils like pinpricks, and I leaned back, both of us now soaking wet under the cascade of frigid water. Gradually the color began returning to his cheeks.

"W-what happened?" he croaked.

I ignored him and went out to change my soiled bedding. By the time I came back into the bathroom, the shower was off, and he was at the sink staring in the mirror. I handed him his phone.

"Call your men," I instructed. "Tell them to wait outside the gate when they arrive." He looked afraid, but we didn't have time. "Here," I said more gently, offering him a glass of water. "Drink, you'll feel better."

"But the G . . ." He looked up at me, suddenly a six-year-old scared of his parents.

"I'm a doctor," I lied, betting that in that state he would believe whatever I told him. "I'm not sure what exactly you took, but you need to go a hospital immediately. Do you understand me?"

He blinked once and nodded.

"Good. Now, call your men. Tell them that you need to see a doctor for dehydration. You'll be fine. It'll be fine."

He nodded again. After some minutes he gathered himself enough to concoct a story on the phone about having a reaction to a bad samosa. Moments later there was a knock on my gate, and I opened it to see three men waiting in crisp, freshly pressed uniforms.

"Cheese samosas," I trilled, and pushed his unsteady form over toward them. "Who knew mozzarella could expire? Hahaha!"

They took him without expression, and it only occurred to me then that this was probably not his first time being hauled out of a stranger's house high on GHB. As I watched the car drive away, my body released the panic it had been stockpiling for the past hour. I was in the middle of pouring myself a shaky measure of bright blue gin when my phone lit up. The text was from one of the few gay men in Lahore who had made it to their early thirties without getting married or engaged to a woman (that he designed wedding gowns is an altogether different crisis).

"Your Grindr pictures are on Instagram!" the text said. "Please report the account now before someone sees it! Goes by Munda666. He's got everyone on there. Spread the word!"

I followed the link to an Instagram account titled @gaysofpakistanigrindr. The tagline *Exposing immorality* loomed above a profile photo of a vengeful crescent moon floating above a grid of hazy squares, each a screenshot of private pictures surreptitiously saved from vulnerable conversations. I recognized my own form, third from the top, staring back from behind a well-placed shampoo bottle.

Could be worse, I thought, downing the last of my blue gin. *At least I have the most likes.*

The account was taken down some weeks later, coincidentally the same day I finally heard from Sebastian's brother. Yes, the patient was doing better. No, he likely would not be allowed to go back home for some months. Yes, they've been getting my messages. No, he has not been given his phone back yet. Yes, he's been asking about me. Yes, I may talk to him at some point in the future. No, we don't know when. Yes, we'll keep in touch, but don't keep contacting us, please. The family has enough to deal with at the moment. Thank you. Goodbye.

Chapter 15

RETURN TO OZ

T HE INCIDENTS OF THE BREAKDOWN, the officer, and the Instagram (sounds like a revenge porn murder mystery, I know) coincided with a string of other attacks on my mental health. My family's enduring commitment to ignoring my sexuality meant that confiding in them about my pain felt not only futile but dangerous. I ignored my pain and threw myself into work, and three months later debuted a depressing series of paintings showing solitary figures trapped in oceans of gold leaf. Just after the opening, I collapsed unconscious on the floor.

"Could be dengue fever," a silver-haired doctor told me after I woke up in a peeling hospital ward that smelled like hemorrhoid ointment. One of my arms was hooked up to an IV drip while the other swatted away a court of mosquitoes that had mistaken me for their queen. "But it could also be malaria, or hepatitis A, or scarlet fever, or Zika virus. One never knows these days."

"Shouldn't one, though, given one's medical degree?"

Great, I thought as he laughed his way out of the ward, *it's like playing Russian roulette, except instead of bullets, I get a buffet of subtropical diseases and a free stay at the Hospice Inn.* Two weeks later my yellow skin made it clear I had developed jaundice, probably from drinking contaminated water (hope springs eternal but also unfiltered). Sickeningly weak but verifiably thin, I finally achieved my lifelong goal weight for a grand total of twelve days and seventeen hours before I discovered I could digest dairy again. I was also finally able to quit cigarettes for good, but my heady euphoria was tempered by an ailing liver and the infuriating realization that even at the slimmest I'd been since kindergarten, my breasts remained, like Pakistan itself, stubbornly resilient. But my extreme physical illness did bring on a certain bright clarity as I lay on that ratty hospital mattress: If I wanted to live my full life authentically, one where I could find a partner who loves me, a career that fulfills me, and a home that shelters all parts of my life, I couldn't do it here.

After nearly five years, it was time to leave Pakistan.

I emailed the lawyers from my sickbed, and they defrosted my dormant immigration application. Over the next several weeks, I sent in reams of documentation gingerly saved over the past half decade: show invitations, art reviews, news articles, my weekly columns, letters of recommendation, the eligible bachelors list, even a screenshot of that one time my art website was hacked by a trio of Bangladeshi teenagers for "bringing dishonor on Islam," which was more irritating than actually dangerous, given that I'd just sent the link to an enthusiastic foreign gallerist who, quite understandably, ghosted me hard afterward. Strangely, there was no dread or anxiety about the outcome of my application this time around, just an overwhelming sense of knowing this was meant to be. Some months later I woke up to an email with a short subject heading:

Approved

I went numb. The news I had been approved for a green card felt too monumental, too life-changing for a single word to convey. I spent the next day weeping in relief and the next week floating on a cloud.

It may sound like I casually popped into the local post office on my way to the gym to pick up a green card, but that is usually only true of white people moving from Canada. For the rest of the world, the process of immigrating to the United States is a slow, stressful, often fruitless plod through the marsh pit of chance, circumstance, and hope. But I had made it! And through all the subsequent red tape that immigrating to America involves—the status adjustments, the embassy interviews, the rectal exams—I remained completely, utterly, and fundamentally bewildered at my change in fortune. Getting the green card felt like a universal vindication, the easing of a burden of self-doubt I'd carried ever since the Academy, the one that whispered constantly in my ear: *You'll never be good enough.*

Approved!

I was particularly smug to have reached this milestone on the strength of my own talents. It had not come to me by way of a marriage of convenience or a corporate job (though one of the lessons life eventually teaches you is that nobody gives you marks for doing it the hard way). The United States of America wanted me for me and, like Molly Ringwald at the end of *Sixteen Candles*, I felt blessed and highly favored. This time, unburdened of the stress of imminent deportation, I'd finally be able to build a permanent life for myself.

APPROVED!

Tariq was devastated, but once I got him to stop crying long enough to hear that he'd still be employed to look over my place in my absence, he cheered right up. A witch in Mumbai once told me to be intentional about dates in my life, so I purposely timed my reentry into America to coincide with Halloween (ever a gay high holiday), but sadly, travel delays meant I spent Halloween night on a stained mattress at a Qatari airport hotel hate-scrolling through pictures of peoples' costumes. I arrived in New York as permanent resident on November 1, 2015.

"Is that really you?" my Airbnb host asked as I taped a photo of my teenage self on the fridge of the Brooklyn apartment I had sublet for my first few months.

"Some of me," I said, and explained how I used the picture as a deterrent to late-night snacking.

"You *do* look like a fat Aladdin in that T-shirt," she said, leaning in to study the photograph.

"You look like a crack whore Jasmine in those pants," I replied reflexively. Later, as I watched her hurry back to her car in tears, I did actually spot a lady dressed in a Princess Jasmine costume emerge from a run-down apartment building across the street. "Ah," I sighed, as a fat rat chased Jasmine around the street corner. "New York!"

It was the small things: the fact that the air quality wasn't hazardously polluted every morning; that the electricity didn't arbitrarily disappear at odd hours; that there was always gas in the stove no matter the time of the day; the hard-won knowledge that when people asked for my pictures on Grindr it probably wasn't because they were running an anonymous account to out gay men. Away from the unrelenting pressure of surviving daily life in Lahore, life on the stability of my green card felt quietly spacious. It was time to start building. I rented a small art studio in Bushwick and slowly began reintroducing myself to New York City. The wounds from the end of my relationship with Sebastian were far from healed, but slowly, gradually, I was able to move beyond the fact of my pain.

America felt like a different country to the one I had left years ago: The NSEERS program had been abolished ("Sorry 'bout that," a customs officer said at the airport), the wars on terror were now a traumatic memory buttressed by communal amnesia, and *RuPaul's Drag Race* was a cultural phenomenon. At the tail end of the Obama years, people seemed hopeful and confident. But grateful as I was for another chance at life in America, I was still weary from my last stint. Two Republican presidencies, three foreign wars, and a Muslim registration program are not things one easily forgets.

The summer of 2015, when I was approved for my green card, was also the summer the US Supreme Court legalized gay marriage and, with it, changed the world for millions of us queers. The court ruling was a legal declaration of the inviolable right of being myself, an institutionalized benediction that made my search for love legal in America and, quietly but consequentially, everywhere American culture existed. If American law now recognized gay marriage, that meant its citizens were also now bound to protect that fact in embassies across the homophobic world. America was exporting gay rights as well as procedural medical dramas.

The flip side of the court ruling was that American gay men, mostly white ones, began talking about gay rights with a renewed abstraction, as an issue solved rather than an ongoing global crisis. The American queer community had spent the sixties marching for visibility, the seventies marching for freedom, and the eighties marching for dignity. Many brave people of all different creeds and colors were responsible for those vital early battles, but most courtroom plights for gay recognition in America in the eighties and nineties were undertaken by well-heeled white gay men, mostly by virtue of their money and influence. Now, after all the devastation the HIV pandemic had wreaked, those same white men wanted nothing more than to blend back into the majority. Characters like Mitch and Cam from *Modern Family* were created to declare, *We are like you, just another family with kids and a white picket fence.* Because we are like you, mainstream gayness told middle America, it's OK for you to like us.

But the elasticity of institutional tolerance in America rarely, if ever, stretches to include people of color. That's the thing about the American dream: You have to be asleep to believe it. The exported version of the United States I saw on screens growing up outside the country was not the lived reality of those inside it. Much like Lady Chancery or *khala* Boob stratified people based on wealth and lineage, America ranked people based on proximity to whiteness—in either color, caste, or culture. Homosexuality is an exception to this stratification because gay sex can cut through most barriers of race, class, and education that order us. Sometimes this apparent malleability can mislead us into mislabeling all queer activists as one homogenous group with unified priorities, empathy, and awareness. From my own experience, I know this is not true.

The machine that fought for marriage equality had many moving parts, but that marriage equality was the biggest priority at all is largely because white people made it so. By far the world's most successful racial movement, white supremacy works tirelessly to protect its own. The fight for marriage equality was a large enough bandwagon to include some social conservatives precisely because it conformed neatly to that most heteronormative of all family structures, i.e., wedded union. The march for gay marriage was always a march for assimilation, but what people missed is that America mostly only assimilated white gays.

Within a year of my arrival, two things happened that made this intersectional sense of alienation conspicuous. One was the 2016 presidential election, when America elected a president who wore racism, hairpieces, and a cadmium-orange spray tan with equal enthusiasm. The other took place six months before, in what was America's largest public shooting massacre at the time.

On the evening of June 12, 2016, Omar Mateen, the American-born shooter of Afghani origin, entered Pulse nightclub in Orlando. By the end of the night he had murdered forty-nine people and injured another fifty. It was horrific.

The news coverage of the massacre quickly became binary: "Islamic Radical Terrorists Hatred for Gays Fueled Massacre!" The unsurprising effort to use the slaughter as yet another justification for America's continual war with Islam abroad felt terrifyingly familiar. It was rooted, partly, in something we now call homonationalism, the comparatively new phenomenon by which countries brandish their adoption of gay rights as a barometer of their enlightenment that can, consequently, act as a camouflage for other forms of bigotry they may actively foster.

Almost immediately, mainstream media used the shooter's Muslim identity to vilify Islam, Afghans, and Muslim immigrants as a whole. Much of the nuance the media typically affords to white shooters in America, whose high school experiences and mental illnesses are dutifully recounted and dolefully deconstructed as if the very notion of violence itself is non-white, didn't extend to this incident. Someone like Mateen was not another in a long line of disgruntled men with mental issues who had committed mass murder aided by America's gun laws. No, he was an Afghan export, a Muslim agent, a foreign problem. There was no outcry over the arcane laws that allowed a man previously reported to the FBI to buy that much ammunition; it didn't matter to the pundits that Mateen was likely gay himself, or that the terrorist groups he was mistakenly associated with existed in direct opposition to each other. All that mattered was that the culprit had a Muslim name, which allowed people to use this tragedy to resurrect the image of a civilized America fighting against the savagery of Islamic ideology. America, of course, had no Christian homophobes or white mass murderers. And Muslims—no matter the details of their personal faith—were expected to denounce the act of violence like decentralized spokespeople. To relive a national reenactment of the same knee-jerk Islamophobia that had colored so much of my first stint in the United States felt triggering, except this time the rhetoric of us-versus-them had been brought into my specific corner of a safe space. *Gay or Muslim.*

As a Muslim, I felt scared. As a gay man, I felt terrified. As a gay Muslim immigrant male, I bought full-fat ice cream.

The only downside to the Marriage Equality Act was that every date I went on now had the threat of marriage hiding behind every hors d'oeuvres. The pain of being with Sebastian had taught me that I wanted a partner as publicly invested in their authenticity as I was, and so clandestine Grindr hookups gave way to expensive Tinder outings at fancy restaurants with men who were looking to date rather than simply hook up.

Wonderful though some of those evenings were, I found it difficult to pretend that the reality of gay Manhattan was the only one I inhabited. When I spoke to the Davids, Christophers, and, yes, even the Hunters, about my life, it was with some measure of irritation that I found myself having to explain what living and loving in a country that doesn't have gay rights could feel like.

"That's wild," Hunter said on our second date. "I could never grow up in a place like that."

What makes you think you didn't? Places like the West Village, West Hollywood, and Chicago's Boystown were singular enclaves in an otherwise vast territory of red hats, conversion therapists, Baptist rage, and puritan revulsion. Homophobia didn't simply evaporate in America with a supreme court ruling any more than racism did with the election of her first Black president.

But Hunter, a corporate PR associate whose mother had thrown him a *Jem and the Holograms*–themed coming-out party at thirteen, didn't want to hear that, anxious as he was to dismiss my opinions as the bitter ramblings of a repressed self-hating queer from Wher-everistan. Hunter was eager to start playing happy family, spending evenings debating the virtues of adoption versus surrogacy or which *RuPaul's Drag Race* queen should be canceled next. I envied his sense of aculturalism but found it hard to imagine taking him (or any of my other suitors) back to Pakistan one day. After all this time, the hyphens of my identity felt less like bridges than barriers. Would I always have to disregard some vital part of myself to find love?

Fuck no, I thought as Hunter told me yet another party story about fitness models doing molly. If I had refused to conform to unhappiness for my family in Pakistan, I sure as shit wasn't about to start doing it for a PR associate from Idaho.

America elected Trump a year after my arrival (yes, moving to America then felt like crashing a New Year's Eve party at four A.M.), but it was, despite the general depression, a mild relief to see some Americans begin to discover the hypocrisy of their national image. This time of strife felt different from the Bush years because there was at least some dissent from the Democrats, many of whom had been so patriotically silent before. Still, I was more irritated than assuaged by the performative outrage of left-leaning white liberals in the aftermath of what became four years of daily Republican fascistic aggressions.

"Can you believe Trump is trying to ban Muslims from America?" I was often asked by white Democrats at brownstone dinner parties. For them, the recent attacks on America's international image from its president were somehow entirely separate from the country they felt they knew. It took every reserve of strength I had not to slap them across the cheek, Alexis Carrington–style, as I screamed, "HOW DID YOU NOT REALIZE THIS AFTER INVADING EVERY COUN-TRY BUT THE ONE THAT SENT THE 9/11 TERRORISTS, YOU OIL-CENTRIC, UNINFORMED HYPOCRITE!"

Sorry, sometimes sitting inside a fog of other people's entitlement can make one lightheaded. Any one of us who endured NSEERS knows that what is shocking is not that the Republican Trump admin-istration tried to ban Muslims; it was that so many well-meaning Americans had forgotten that the country already had.

Chapter 16

HELLO, GORGEOUS!

*H*E WAS HALF-PERUVIAN, HALF-GREEK, WORKED at the UN, spoke six languages, and looked like a rugged carpenter dressed by Dior. We met on Tinder, and by date two I was already googling *scenic tuscan wedding packages*. But by date four we still hadn't slept together, which is one of the drawbacks of imitative heteronormative gay dating apps like Tinder, where an altogether false sense of modesty takes over gay men who would otherwise happily have sent you closeups of their prostate on any other platform.

Sadly, my manboobs had returned with a buoyant vengeance (Trader Joe's soft-cheese aisle). But despite that, my body image was on a rare upswing because of a recent discovery I had made in the basement at Macy's: Spanx. Men don't talk about them enough, but Spanx are transcendental, magical creations. Essentially very tight underwear that forces your body fat into a temporary state of compliance at the expense of your internal organs, they are indispensable for that potent sense of delusional confidence only medical-grade polyester can provide.

He said work was busy, so I didn't worry when he ignored my swooning texts all week. I imagined him sitting at his office over the

East River solving world hunger for lunch before attacking global poverty, effortlessly switching between Portuguese and Swahili as he negotiated trade deals with distant dignitaries. What a dinner guest he would make! Worldly but not jaded, foreign but familiar. Mother would *love* him!

When he texted suggesting last-minute drinks suspiciously near his Brooklyn apartment, I knew that would be the night we'd finally have sex. I primped and preened for three hours while rehearsing my wedding toast ("First off, thank you to everyone for making it to Capri on such short notice . . .") and ran over as fast as my corsetry allowed. The drinks went well (one always comes to life under the threat of sex), but it wasn't until we were making out in his bed later that the unavoidable implications of my physical deception became mournfully clear.

"Wow, that's . . . really tight," he said, tugging hard to dislodge my stomach from its binding scaffolding.

"Just an undershirt," I muttered. I tried sucking in my stomach to create more space but that only made the shapewear recoil tighter, like a cruel Chinese finger trap.

"Like, *really* tight. What—Jesus!—what is that made of?"

When I finally stumbled into shirtlessness, a look of undiluted disappointment unfurled across his face like a postapocalyptic sunset.

Fifteen minutes of aimless, unenthusiastic groping followed.

"You're not into this," I said eventually. He looked genuinely relieved to stop.

"I'm sorry. I don't know what to say. I guess I didn't expect . . ."

I was propped up on my elbow and could feel the weight of my left tit hanging off my chest, so I sat up against the headboard. "Go on," I said, covering my nipples with a pillow. "It's OK. Tell me."

"I don't think we are a match. Physically," he added, a somewhat unnecessary lemon slice wedged into the gaping wound of my self-esteem.

"Yeah!" I said, already hopping around the room trying to find my pants. "Course! Totally!" I reached down for my shirt and caught a glimpse of myself in a full-length mirror. The streetlamp just outside the window cast an eerie, unflattering yellow glow over the entire bedroom. I looked like Big Bird after chemo.

He kept staring at me as I silently dressed. Maybe he felt bad about how this had ended, maybe he was just counting the seconds until I was finally out the door and he could log on to get off. I compensated for the painful awkwardness by projecting Tibetan happiness. No, of course I'm fine. Yes, I'm sure! We're both adults after all. Yes, I'd love to go with you to the Picasso retrospective next week. Yes, as friends, obviously! *deranged laughter* Great! Text you soon. Good night!

I cried the whole subway ride back into Manhattan, the wilted spandex stuffed into the back pocket of my date-night jeans. As the L train jostled from Brooklyn to Fourteenth Street, I stared down at the folds of my rejected body, this pudgy prison that had been the cause and caucus of so much of my anguish. I couldn't remember a meal in my life I hadn't admonished myself for eating or wondered how many calories it cost me afterward. There hadn't been a day since puberty that I didn't tug at my T-shirt to create space for my chest, or spend that extra half hour changing outfits, refusing to leave the house until I found a pair of clothes that made me feel presentable. Not attractive, mind you. Presentable.

Why isn't my body enough? I thought, glaring at the young gay couple making out opposite me on the subway. I was sick of feeling inadequate, but it couldn't be mere coincidence that the moments when I had been at my thinnest were also when I was at my unhappiest. I remember once being confident enough to tuck my shirt inside my pants before one of my art openings, a memory stored in the vault not because of how good it felt to have finally achieved that milestone, but because of how bad I felt that I still felt bad. No matter what I did to my body, in my mind I was still that overweight, effeminate boy afraid of being ridiculed at the pool.

A month later I went on a holiday in Greece, during which I didn't take off my shirt once without shame. Despite that, I spent my last night in a hotel with an Athenian man I'd met at the beach who looked like a sculpture with a spray tan. Adonis (seriously) turned out to be so mind-numbingly good in bed that I later took out cash from my backpack in case he handed me a bill for services rendered. Luckily, Adonis (but, like, seriously) appeared to like me for me, and over breakfast the next morning we exchanged email addresses. On my flight back home, my mind kept wrestling with the paralyzing fear of ridicule and self-doubt that being intimate with someone that beautiful still brought up inside me.

But something was different this time, like the moment in a dream when you realize you are dreaming. I felt ashamed of myself after the UN man rejected me, yes, but I also felt ashamed after a Greek god gave me four orgasms in two hours. Something didn't add up here. And in the minuscule amount of space that this illogical incongruity created, I was able to see for the first time that my self-hatred was a creature utterly separate from me as a person. Cruel, ugly, and violent, it was a feral pet I'd unwittingly housed deep inside my psyche for decades. Suddenly I felt the weight of its frothing hate on my soul, the crushing pain of the putrefying, toxic poison I actively imbibed every time I wrongly equated any negative thoughts with indisputable fact.

It didn't have to be this way. *You've done extraordinary things*, I told myself, relishing this unfamiliar sense of inner confidence. *You lost weight when you wanted to, made a career out of something you love, and manifested a green card into existence out of thin air. You've confronted rejection, suicide, homophobia, heartbreak, depression, assault, insults, and silence. And still here you are.*

And you are resplendent.

What was the point of carrying all this self-hatred around? How many pelvic-shattering orgasms had I missed because of the heaviness of my own baggage? How much happiness and joy? How many appetizers and desserts?

It was a stunning, slightly nauseating realization, if only for its clichéd simplicity, because if I was the one who carried the baggage, that meant I could also put it down. If I disliked a part of my body so much that I put life itself on perpetual hold, then I could change it. Through diet, through exercise, through surgery, through any way I deemed, for lack of a better term, fit. I woke up from a nap on the flight back with a freeing decision already resting in glamorous repose in the sunken couch of my mind, as fully formed as the goddess Athena herself.

It's been long enough, Athena said. *Nix the tits.*

I'd had surgery once before, an emergency appendectomy when I was ten. Right before that operation, I'd watched an episode of *The Oprah Winfrey Show* about a then-new procedure called liposuction. The doctor on TV demonstrated how he could vacuum out fat from specific trouble spots with no more effort than the push of a button.

"Just like that?" I asked the TV, a string of mozzarella dangling from my mouth.

"Just like that!" the doctor told Oprah, waving a turkey baster in the air with a flourish. "Gone forever!"

Forever.

Liposuction was a conceptual game changer. The hope that I could one day have my fat sucked out of me became the subconscious reason I'd go on to resist salads, exercise, and portion control throughout puberty. *As God as my witness*, I thought as I was rushed into the operation theater, *I'll never have love handles again!* But sadly, the doctors remained defiantly unresponsive to my requests for elective plastic surgery no matter how many times I jiggled my tits at them, and I left the hospital five days later cut up but nowhere near ripped. But the germ of the idea never really went away, unlike my appendix.

After accompanying me through all these years, you probably think my decision to finally do something about my chesticles should unfold like a biblical revelation: me standing in Renaissance ecstasy as a pair of giant boobs floated above me on puffy clouds, each tit held up by cabal of struggling cherubs bathed in golden light and accompanied by a sweeping orchestral score. If it helps, the fact that after twenty years of diets, treadmills and Betty Crocker binge cycles, the answer to my genetic plight had only been an internet search away was infuriating to me too.

Please welcome to the stage . . . gynecomastia!

boos

"Gynecomastia," Dr. Jacobstein explained at my initial examination, "is a medical condition that causes increased breast tissue in men. It usually runs in families and, to answer your question, no, there is no way you can get rid of it without surgery." I choked back tears. "No amount of diet or exercise could ever have removed it completely . . . it's not, erm, your fault, you know?" He looked visibly uncomfortable as I wept. "You just have to have them surgically removed."

And so I did. In the words of our shaman RuPaul: "If you can't love yourself, how in the hell you gonna love somebody else?"

"Ready?" the anesthesiologist asked, and before I could say, "Fuck no," a wave of euphoria carried me off to a happy place far, far away. There was no sound here, nor any pain. It was warm and cozy, and in the distance, I saw something glowing bright red. As I approached, the glow revealed itself to be a stage curtain, and no sooner did the thought cross my mind than a comfortable seat appeared behind me. The curtains opened to reveal a bright stage bathed in a warm light. The faint sound of a choir came from a far distance. Or was it *qawaals*? Gold glitter rained down, and I looked up to see *khala* Boob balancing on a trapeze near the ceiling like an AARP cabaret act. The heft of my late great-aunt was squeezed into a tiny, bejeweled corset that cinched her waist into nothingness and sent her majestic boobs rising up like the Himalayas themselves.

God, I thought as *khala* Boob descended toward me, *she looks spectacular*. And no sooner had her stripper heels touched the stage floor than there was an explosion of gold dust and my great-aunt was transformed in an instant into a single, angry breast. The breast reclined back on a red Victorian chaise in regal splendor and exhaled a puff of smoke. Somehow, I knew we belonged to each other.

"So," my left boob said. "This is it, then."

I nodded.

"Will it make a difference?"

"I hope so."

Another explosion and my right boob joined us, both tits now dressed in matching gold sequined jackets and top hats. The faint sound of the opening bars of a familiar musical came from a great distance.

"We didn't mean to hurt you," my right boob said.

"I know." I said, feeling a sudden surge of affection for that which I was about to lose. The music got louder. "I'm sorry I was mean to you for so long."

My manboobs rose in unison.

"See you in your sixties," they said, standing together like conjoined twins. Another burst of confetti as the music reached a crescendo, and the stage was now full of all sorts of breasts: big, small, round, flat, pendulous, pert, male, female, hairy, heaving, all of them dancing with their little arms interlocked and their legs swinging like the Rockettes. I saw *khala* Boob above, laughing as she flew across stage on her trapeze, this time dressed in a leopard-print leotard and a tiara of red ostrich plumes. After quite an impressive display of upper-body strength, she swung down close to me once more.

"Be happy," she said, touching my cheek. I smiled and nodded, and the swing whisked her away as a chorus line of breasts followed her off stage in synchronized formation.

"Thank you!" I wanted to shout out, but my voice had left me.

The music died down, and one last breast turned to face me on the now empty stage.

"Komail," it said gently. "Time to wake up now."

My throat felt raw.

"Yes, that's it. Good . . . good, open your eyes." The doctor's voice was deep and soothing. "The operation was a complete success!"

"Promise?" I croaked.

"Promise."

The surgery took two hours and cost me all my savings. My left boob weighed 4 pounds, my right 3.8 pounds. It was a simple enough procedure that they discharged me the same day and so, regretfully, I didn't get the chance to perform the monologue from *Wit* I'd memorized to entertain myself in the hospital room.

"Where the fuck is the fucking Uber?" Noor swore as we stood outside the surgeon's office on Seventy-Third Street and Park Avenue. He was still my emergency contact, and both he and Ayaan had volunteered to care for me after the operation. It had been over a year since they told me they had feelings for each other. They lived as a couple now, the fulfillment of a silent pledge of affection that I knew stretched back to our days at the Academy.

"Are you feeling OK?" Noor said.

I groaned in flat-chested agony.

"Sit down on the bench. The car will be here any minute."

As I looked down at the flatness of my bandaged torso, I felt a relief I cannot describe fully enough in words or paint. A deep calm seeped into me over the weeks of my convalescence, a rightness of being in my body that I had never felt before. After I healed, very few people noticed the change unless I told them, which is as good a sign as any that most of your worst fears only exist in your mind. But they did notice the rise in my confidence as I took deliberate steps to confront all the things in my life that my body dysmorphia had kept me afraid of: shirtlessness, gay beaches, linen tops against strong winds, the Cheesecake Factory, love.

When I arrived at the doctor's office a year later for my final check-up I noticed a fat pigeon fly down to rest on the green and white signage for Park Avenue and Seventy-Third Street outside the building. And I smiled and hummed the tune of a prophetic lullaby from a childhood long ago: "Grab a cab, c'mon see the wizard on Park and Seventy-Third for tits and ass!"

Chapter 17

GOING ON EIGHTEEN . . .

Please raise your right hand. Do you swear to tell the truth, the whole truth, and nothing but the truth?
I do, sir.

Take a seat. Do you understand that this is an interview concerning your application to become a US citizen?
Yes, sir.

How long have you been in the United States as a permanent resident?
Six years now, sir.

You don't have to call me sir.
Are you sure?

Please, call me Gary. What is your profession?
I'm an artist. And a writer.

And what kind of art do you make?
Mostly paintings, but for the last several years I've been working on a book about growing up gay in Pakistan.

That's great! What's it called?
Manboobs.

Man . . . ?
Boobs. Yes.

That's quite a title.
Thank you, Gary. I wanted to call it *Manboobs: A Tale of Two Titties*, but no one let me.

Obviously I worried having any kind of cosmetic procedure would awaken the surgery addict within me who, once roused from her anesthetized slumber, would force me into endless facelifts until my face too resembled a cat trapped in a high-speed wind tunnel. That didn't happen, mostly because a euphoric sense of belonging in one's own body is as short-lived as any joy you do not actively nurture. And while the gynecomastia surgery didn't eliminate the cruelty of my inner monologues (a voice still whispers "tummy tuck" to me in my dreams), it did provide me with verifiable proof that they were mostly noise.

I think often of an email Sebastian wrote to me in which he said that while the voices in his head never stopped speaking, he had, slowly, learned to ignore them.

I see from your travel history that you regularly visited Pakistan during the last five years. Was that for work or family?
A little of both. My family lives there.

Always good to see family.
Yes, Gary.

"You're going to have to make a choice," I finally said to my mother on a trip to Lahore. My parents were older now, less interested in the world than in their memories of it. I had worked hard to include them in my life, but my sexuality still remained, after all these years, a topic of silence.

"You can accept that I am gay," I said, "or we can agree to stop meeting each other. But I'm not going to keep pretending for you anymore. One way or another, it's time for a choice."

She considered me from behind her book, her face lined and fuller now, that thin eyebrow still arched high. I met her gaze evenly. I was no longer the guilty child convinced that hiding my sexuality was the only way to keep my family whole. In the years of purgatory I spent between permanent resident and American citizen, I had slowly melded the fractured pieces of myself into a more cohesive whole. My work—painting and writing both—bloomed once I rooted them in the honesty I had deliberately avoided for years. I was done hiding. From them, from Pakistan, from the world. I'd spent so much of my life waiting for someone else's approval that it never occurred to me to ask whether, after all this time, I needed anyone's but my own. No, this was not about approval. This was about inclusion. This was about a choice.

"A choice about what?" Ma asked.

"About whether you hate my being gay more than you love me."

I'd expected her to deny it, to tell me how crazy I was for imagining a bigotry that had simply never existed, and it was a twisted kind of relief when she said instead: "I can't do that."

"It's who I am."

"But it's not the *only* thing you are!" she cried. And for one brief, honest moment I saw the mask of her invulnerability slip down to reveal the scared child hiding behind it. I saw then how deeply she loved me, how terrified she was of losing me, and how incapable she was of doing anything to prevent it. "There is so much *more* to you than just . . . just *that*!"

It took some effort to keep my voice calm as I sat opposite her. "It doesn't work that way," I said. "You can't pick and choose the parts of me you love. I'm happy, and I'm asking you to accept all of me—not Pakistan, or strangers, or religious zealots—but you, my family." She looked like she'd swallowed disappointment dipped in lemon juice, but I pressed on: "But if you can't do that, that's fine too." And as I studied the deep furrows of her disapproving brow, I noticed my father's shadow under the door as he eavesdropped on us from the next room, and I suddenly felt sorry for us all. "I'm proud of myself," I said, louder now so they could both hear me. "The only question is whether you want to be a part of my life. So, I'll ask you again, please, choose."

"I'm your mother!" she finally said. "What does 'a part of my life' even mean?"

A part. Apart. One joins in separation, the other separates in joining. And even as my mother willfully ignored the fundamental question I put before her, she *was* right in her own way. She was always going to be my mother; that much even language cannot undo. Her reluctance to embrace all of me was as much a part of her as my body had once been; I knew that, just as I knew my father couldn't tell a soul in his life the truth about me. I was beloved in the darkness of secrecy. For some people, it's the only place they can love. I have made peace with that paradox, a fragile barbed peace that soothes and stings. I suspect it always will. Not a day goes by that my longing for the fantasy of a perfect family doesn't overwhelm me. But I know things now that I never knew before, and as much as it hurt me to accept it, it was never in my power to fix what was broken before I was born.

"I'm sorry," she said, "but I'm not making any choice."

I sighed, and walked away, utterly exhausted. "You already have."

A *part, apart*.

Time to begin your civics exam. Who was the first president of the United States?
George Washington.

Name one of the longest rivers in America.
The Mississippi River.

What are the three rights laid out in the Declaration of Independence?
Life, liberty, and the pursuit of happiness!

Who was one of . . . are you all right?
Yes.

Why are you crying?
I'm not crying.

It looks like you're crying . . .
Well, it's just that I think that's lovely.

What is?
That the country was founded for the pursuit of happiness. I mean, isn't that wonderful?

I've been in a long-distance relationship with everything except carbs for most of my adult life. Like hyphens, distance is the price all immigrants pay, and in that way the queer experience and the immigrant experience are twins, for in both we leave one home in search of another. I discovered early that the world treated me differently because of who I might love, so for years I avoided loving at all. Better to be visibly alone in a system I knew than to test how conditional my place inside it really was. Queer people are morosely adept at amputating bits of our souls to fit through narrow doorways. Often it's our only way out alive, but it is no way to live.

It came down to the weight of shame. The shame over how my family might react when I lived my life fully, the shame over how other people might ridicule them if I did, the shame of how faceless strangers would punish me if I refused to capitulate to the idea that my gayness—that I—was only allowed to exist in certain places and in front of certain people. I have known great love after Sebastian too, but I've also learned that relationships—romantic or familial—are not cure-alls. They cannot rescue you, they cannot complete you, and they are only as healthy as the people in them. But it was only when I stopped loving in the shadows that I realized how blasphemous it was for anyone to be ashamed of my love at all. Especially me.

Can you name one of the authors of the Federalist Papers?
Alexander Hamilton!

Please don't sing your answers.
I'm not singing my answers.

It sounds like you're singing them.
Have you seen *Hamilton*? It's a musical about—

Yes, I know what *Hamilton* is about. You're not the first one to mention it today.
I'm not surprised, Gary.

Let's get back to the test. What year was the Declaration of Independence signed?

1776!

You're singing again . . .

∪∿

"Does this color make me look luminous or merely glowy?" Jibran asked as he paraded around our Fire Island rental wearing a bright turquoise kaftan, oversize sunglasses, and a truly enormous straw hat.

"You look great," Noor said, shouting over the sound of a Broadway ballad blaring through the speakers.

Jibran stared at himself in the mirror, unconvinced. "I look like my aunt. Maybe another wig . . . ?" He rummaged through the suitcase of drag he had borrowed from his theatre friend, pulling out swatches of fabric and bits of polyester stockings. "Here, K," he said, throwing a pink-and-white jumble at me. "Something tells me this look is just for you."

I unfolded it to find an elaborate French courtier gown in bright pink taffeta, complete with petticoats, corset, and an ambitiously tall powdered wig.

"Remind me again," Ayaan groaned as Noor struggled to zip him into a lurid mustard-yellow sundress, "why we are doing day drag in July?"

"Because," Jibran said, trying on some lustrous early-Cher hair. "Drag Invasion is far better way to spend the Fourth of July than being forced to watch fireworks with straight people while eating processed meats."

"But what *is* Invasion exactly?" Ayaan asked. "How did it start?"

"Can someone *please* help me with this corset?"

"Gather 'round, children," Jibran said, modulating his voice into that patient tone of polite authority he used with his college students. He helped me into my costume as he recounted the story: "Once upon a July fourth, on a magical gay island of fire not far from New York, there lived a drag queen who needed a drink." He snapped the buttons of my corset shut and bent down to pick up two foam hip cages from the suitcase, which he strapped onto my waist with practiced ease. "But the bartender refused to serve her in drag. Dejected, she sailed back to tell all her friends about what had happened, and they decided to storm the bar in full drag to protest the bartender's narrow-mindedness. The barkeeper, overwhelmed by the parade of fabulous creatures now invading his establishment, apologized profusely and, as a peace offering, gave everyone free drinks for the rest of the night. And so it is," Jibran went on, stuffing a wooden stick into the center of my Marie Antoinette–style wig so that it stood teetering several feet over my head like the leaning tower in Pisa, "that every Fourth of July since then, queer people dress up in drag and 'invade' Fire Island's dock once more, in memory of the battles we have won and—"

"And the drinks we've been searching for ever since?" I finish.

"Amen," Noor said, sitting down in a chic cream dress and pulling out a cigarette.

Jibran stuck several purple ostrich feathers onto the very top of my wig with a flourish and stood back to admire his handiwork. "She's an empress! She's a leader! She's running from the guillotine! Also," he said, turning me around to face the mirror, "she's done . . ."

I stared, transfixed. With the silver high heels, towering white wig, and tiara of ostrich feathers, I stood well over nine feet tall. The white ringlets cascading down my powdered face framed my black beard rather well, much like the purple eyeshadow Noor insisted would accentuate the tiny pink triangle he drew on my cheek. *The gown might not hold up in a historical movie*, I thought, swishing the ruffles of my skirt my from side to side, *but I look deeply fabulous.*

"Time to go!" Noor announced. He and Ayaan went out onto the gray wooden walkway to join the stream of revelers all headed to the main dock, and I gathered up the yards of my gown to join them when I noticed Jibran calling me over.

"I got you a little present," he said, hiding something behind his back. "Well," he added, "not *so* little . . ." He held out the gift in his hands, and it took me a moment to recognize that it was a pair of latex breasts so pendulous that I immediately thought of *khala* Boob. "You're too flat chested now," he said, moving behind to fix the breastplate on me. "At least for today, you need some manboobs back."

I looked at him, too overcome with memory to speak, and he pulled me into as close a hug as the breasts allowed.

"OK! Enough!" He conjured a handkerchief from within his bustline and carefully dabbed his false lashes. "I've spent too much time on my face to ruin it before going out!" He extended a hand. "Shall we dance?"

Outside I tried to keep up pace with everyone, but the opulence of my costume slowed me to a shuffle (you try wearing nine yards of polyblend in July). A strong gust of cool ocean breeze sent the yards of my pink taffeta train billowing out behind me like a gay cloud. "A queen among commoners!" I heard a voice shout from somewhere in the crowd. I tried to trace it and caught a glimpse of my friends strutting ahead with their arms interlocked. Ayaan's heel got caught between the planks of the boardwalk midstep and he suddenly lurched forward, grabbing on to Noor, who screamed and latched on to Jibran, and all three fell into a crumpled heap on the boardwalk, laughing uncontrollably. I smiled, seeing the children we once were and the adults we'd become, and whispered a silent prayer of gratitude for this true moment of happiness, fleeting and perfect.

Good news! I'm recommending you for approval for US citizenship.
Oh my God! Thank you!

**You're very welcome! I'm sorry, no, you're not allowed to hug us.
Yes, behind that line is fine, please. Your oath ceremony will be
scheduled in a few weeks, after which you'll officially become a
citizen of the United States. Do you have any questions?**
I hardly know what to—

Please wait until you are outside the building to sing.
I will, Gary. I promise!

Musicals are how I have ordered my life for as long as I can remember.
That some of the best songs come from hopeless romantics teetering
on the brink of prostitution is only one hint that it's not perfection
that musicals offer but solace. Solace that though no life is without
struggle, no life need be without joy. Being born gay is not a choice,
but it turns out that being happy is. So, I choose happiness over hate,
freedom over falsehood, and celebration over self-censorship. Just as
I chose America—with her messy freedoms, her jaded promises, and
her jagged progress—and she chose me.

But America is bleeding, mortally wounded by the same knife of
white supremacy that fought so long ago to create her. I've seen firsthand what happens to a country when the dullest edges of its society
are sharpened by a group of supremacists to mutilate the body of a
nation. I've lost one home to that fate; I don't want to lose another.

And here we come to the end of my story so far. It is not a fairy
tale, though I found princes. It is not a thriller, though I escaped my
prisons. It is not a musical, though I still belt out ballads unprovoked.
It is a story about being rescued—not by musical fantasies, America,

parental approval, passports, or even love, though those are what I thought I was waiting for, but by, well . . . me.

So please, love yourself first and love yourself well, for one of the shocks on the road to self-acceptance is the discovery that the road never ends. Knowing that and still plodding through its inexhaustible peaks and unfathomable valleys is not an easy thing, it is not painless, but it is, like a good musical, worth it.

ACKNOWLEDGMENTS

"Thank you" feels too light a phrase for the heavy debt of gratitude I carry to the people who helped make this book a reality, but one must begin somewhere. So, please, imagine me crying in couture and clutching a statuette as I weep out my thanks to:

The wonderful Barney Karpfinger at the Karpfinger Agency, for always knowing that this book was more than just a funny read, and for his thoughtful edits on the many drafts I sent over the many years it took to write *Manboobs*.

My incredible literary agent, Sam Chidley, for his intrepid determination, saintly patience, and loyal support. I could not have asked for a better shepherd into the world of publishing.

My fantastic editor, Zack Knoll, for his wit, clarity, and editorial scalpel. Thank you also to Andrew Gibeley, Christian Westermann, and the amazing folks at Abrams Press. It was a joy to work with you. Also, my gratitude to Chelsea Cutchens, for bringing the book to Abrams.

As you know by now, I've lived many lives in many places, always made richer by the presence of people like: Sadia Abbas, Mehr Amin, Isaac Chotiner, Ammara Khalid, the late great Zarina Hashmi, Mina Malik, Allison Nugent, Matthew Phillp, Ayesha Sarfraz, Mira Sethi,

Zainab Shah, Vivien Orbach-Smith, Zohra Rahman, and Dominique Rouleau.

To Alvaro Salas, for his generosity and insight and for giving me a glimpse into a whole new world.

To my sister Momina, for reading early drafts of this book; to Khalid Saeed, for decades of acceptance; to Raeya Saeed and Ramiz Saeed, for their joy and laughter; to my lovely aunt Lalarukh Agha, who first introduced me to musicals; and to my parents, for their love and their art and for showing me what great writing can do.

To Humzah Muzaffar Raja, for being the bravest person I know.

To Veronika Szkudlarek, for her warmth and brilliance.

To Salman Toor, for always being a home.

To Ali Sethi, for his loving generosity.

And to Usman Hamid, for the past thirty years and the many yet to come.

Finally, I want to thank the ten-year-old Komail who still lives within me. He never gave up, even when the rest of me wanted to, and I hope he's as proud of this book as I am of him.

Thank you for reading *Manboobs*. I love you all. Except you wearing the red cardigan. You can do better . . .

ABOUT THE AUTHOR

Komail Aijazuddin is a writer and visual artist. He lives and works in New York City.